GARTH BROOKS
THE ULTIMATE HITS

 Alfred Publishing Co., Inc.
16320 Roscoe Blvd., Suite 100
P.O. Box 10003
Van Nuys, CA 91410-0003
alfred.com

ISBN-10: 1-7390-4950-X
ISBN-13: 978-0-7390-4950-1

CONTENTS

AIN'T GOING DOWN	6
FRIENDS IN LOW PLACES	67
SHAMELESS	174
TWO OF A KIND, WORKIN' ON A FULL HOUSE	202
THE BEACHES OF CHEYENNE	38
IF TOMORROW NEVER COMES	85
PAPA LOVED MAMA	140
MORE THAN A MEMORY	134
GOOD RIDE COWBOY	76
IN ANOTHER'S EYES (The duet with Trisha Yearwood)	92
THE FEVER	58
MIDNIGHT SUN	118
LEARNING TO LIVE AGAIN	100
LONGNECK BOTTLE (Featuring Steve Wariner)	112
TO MAKE YOU FEEL MY LOVE	198
WE SHALL BE FREE	222
THE DANCE	52
CALLIN' BATON ROUGE	19
TWO PIÑA COLADAS	207
THE THUNDER ROLLS	188
THAT SUMMER	159
THE RIVER	150
BEER RUN (The duet with George Jones)	42
UNANSWERED PRAYERS	214
MUCH TOO YOUNG (To Feel This Damn Old)	127
WORKIN' FOR A LIVIN' (The duet with Huey Lewis)	235
WHAT SHE'S DOING NOW	242
WHEN YOU COME BACK TO ME AGAIN (From Frequency)	248
STANDING OUTSIDE THE FIRE	182
AMERICAN HONKY-TONK BAR ASSOCIATION	26
THE CHANGE	48
RODEO	168
WRAPPED UP IN YOU	254
LEAVE A LIGHT ON (Bonus Track)	106

AIN'T GOING DOWN
('TIL THE SUN COMES UP)

Words and Music by
KENT BLAZY, KIM WILLIAMS
and GARTH BROOKS

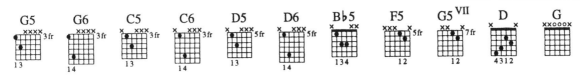

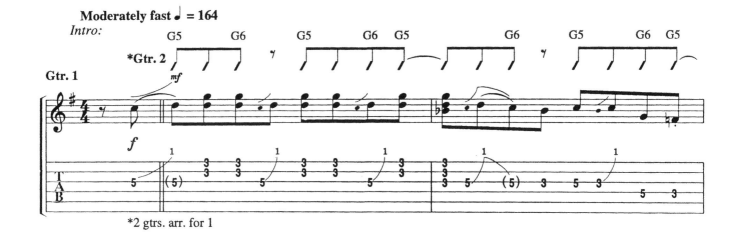

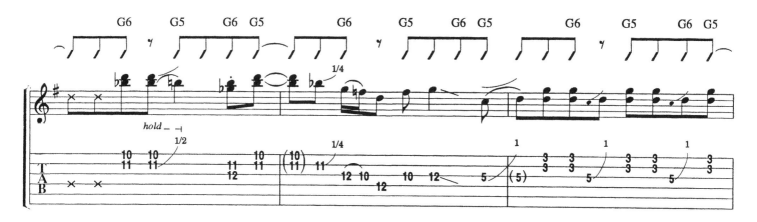

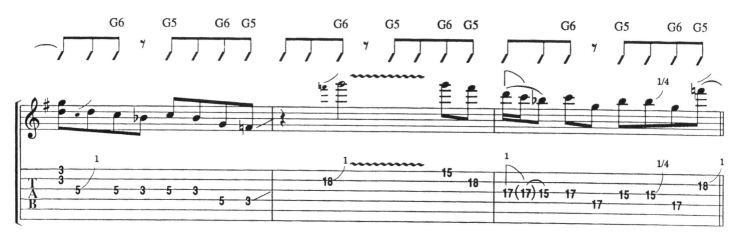

Ain't Going Down ('Til the Sun Comes Up) - 13 - 1
28975

Verse 1 & 2:

8

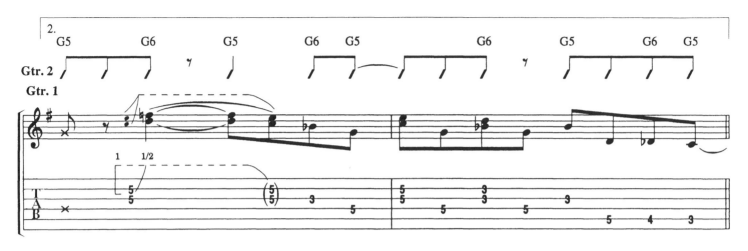

Chorus:

Ain't _ go - ing down 'til the sun comes up. Ain't _____ giv - in' in 'til they

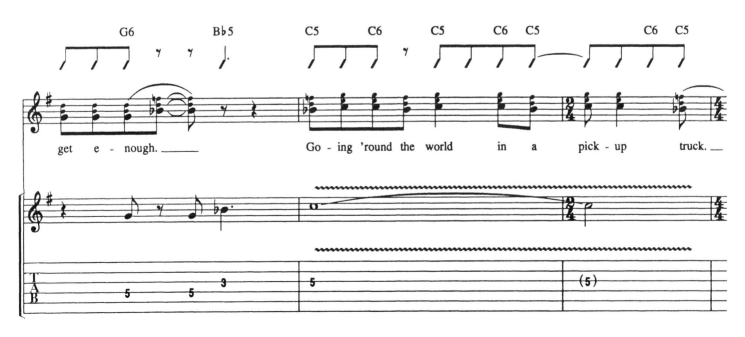

get e - nough. _____ Go - ing 'round the world in a pick - up truck. __

Ain't Going Down ('Til the Sun Comes Up) - 13 - 3
28975

right on where they wan - na be and four o'-clock get up, get go - ing. Five o'-clock that roost-er's crow -

Gtr. 1 & 2

Guitar Solo I:
w/Rhy. Fig. 1 *(Gtrs. 2 & 3, 1 time)*

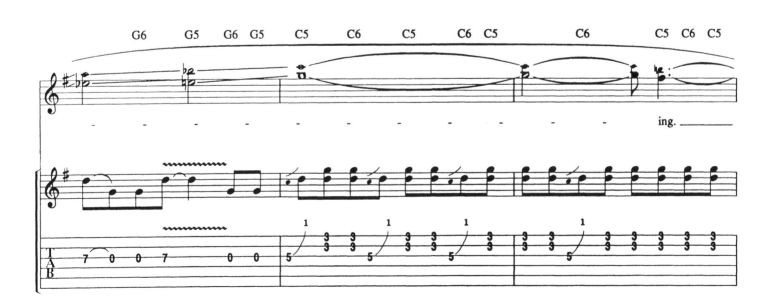

ing. _____

Verse 4:

Six o'-clock on Sat-ur-day, her folks don't know he's on his way. The stalls are clean, the hors-es fed. They

say she's ground-ed 'til she's dead. Well, here he comes, a-round the bend, slow — ing down, she's jump-in' in.

w/Rhy. Fill 1 *(Gtr. 2)*

Hey, mom, your daugh-ter's gone and there they go a-gain._____

Guitar Solo II:
w/Rhy. Fig. 1 *(Gtrs. 2 & 3, 1 time)*

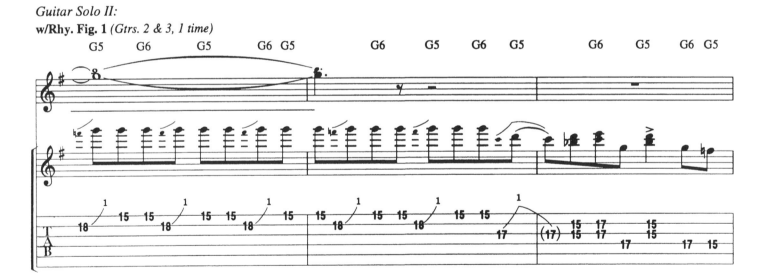

Ain't Going Down ('Til the Sun Comes Up) - 13 - 7
28975

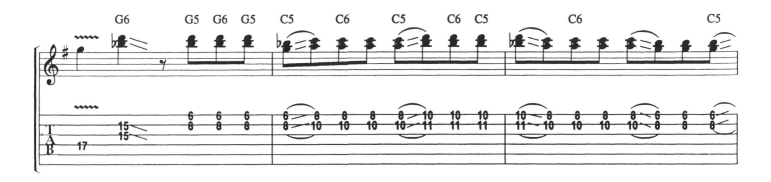

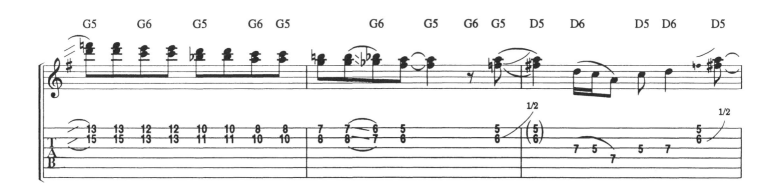

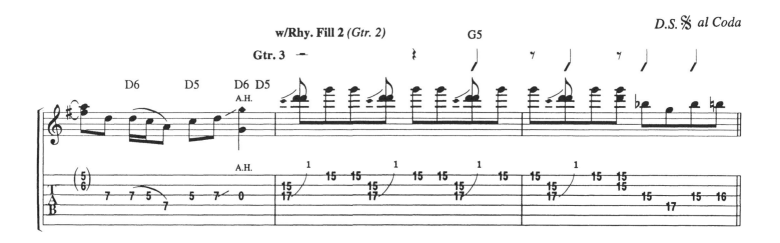

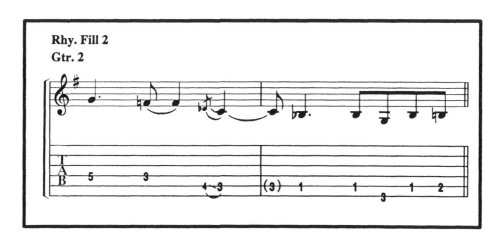

Ain't Going Down ('Til the Sun Comes Up) - 13 - 8
28975

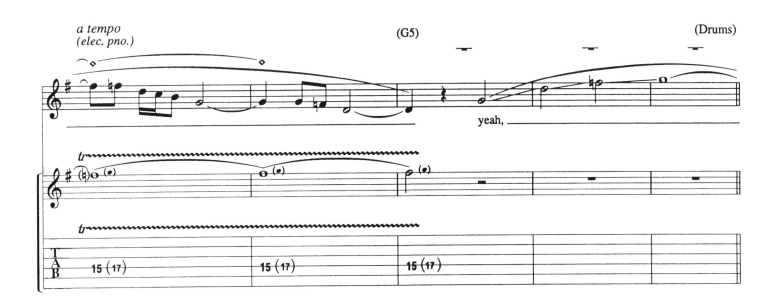

Harmonica Solo II:
w/Rhy. Fig. 1 *(Gtrs. 2 & 3, 1 time)*

Ain't Going Down ('Til the Sun Comes Up) - 13 - 10
28975

*Gtr. 1 "trades 2's" with harmonica while Gtr. 2 improvs. continuously.

Ain't Going Down ('Til the Sun Comes Up) - 13 - 12
28975

18

Outro:
w/Rhy. Fig. 1 *(Gtrs. 2 & 3)*

Verse 2:

Nine o'clock, the show is ending
But the fun is just beginning.
She knows he's anticipating
But she's gonna keep him waiting.
Grab a bite to eat
And then they're headin' to the honky tonk.
But loud crowds and line dancing
Just ain't what they really want.
Drive out to the boondocks and park down by the creek.
And where it's George Strait 'til real late.
And dancing cheek to cheek.

(To Chorus:)

Ain't Going Down ('Til the Sun Comes Up) - 13 - 13
28975

CALLIN' BATON ROUGE

Words and Music by
DENNIS LINDE

†Gtr. II: Banjo, fiddle and dobro arranged for guitar.

1. I spent last night in the arms of a girl in Lou-i-si-an-a,
2. See additional lyrics

*Cue notes are for repeats of Rhy. Fig. 1

Callin' Baton Rouge - 7 - 1
28975

and though I'm out on the high - way— my thoughts— are_____ still— with her.—

Such a strange com - bi - na - tion— of a wom - an and— a child.

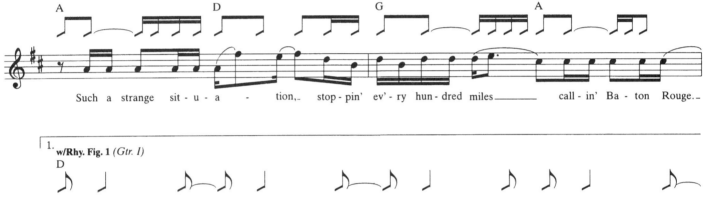

Such a strange sit - u - a - tion,— stop - pin' ev' - ry hun - dred miles_____ call - in' Ba - ton Rouge.—

1.
w/Rhy. Fig. 1 *(Gtr. I)*

Riff A
Gtr. II

(end Riff A)

24

Verse 2:
A replay of last night's events
Roll through my mind.
Except a scene or two
Erased by sweet red wine.
And I see a truck stop sign ahead
So I change lanes.
I need a cup of coffee
And a couple dollars change.
Callin' Baton Rouge.

(To Chorus:)

AMERICAN HONKY-TONK BAR ASSOCIATION

Words and Music by
JIM RUSHING and BRYAN KENNEDY

* Drop ⑥ string to D w/ or w/o D tuner.
  Alternative: Double Gtr. II in unison.

† return ⑥ to E

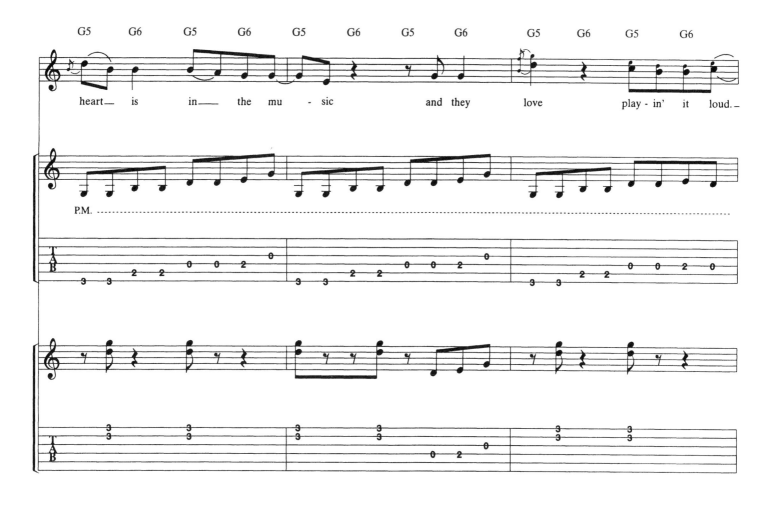

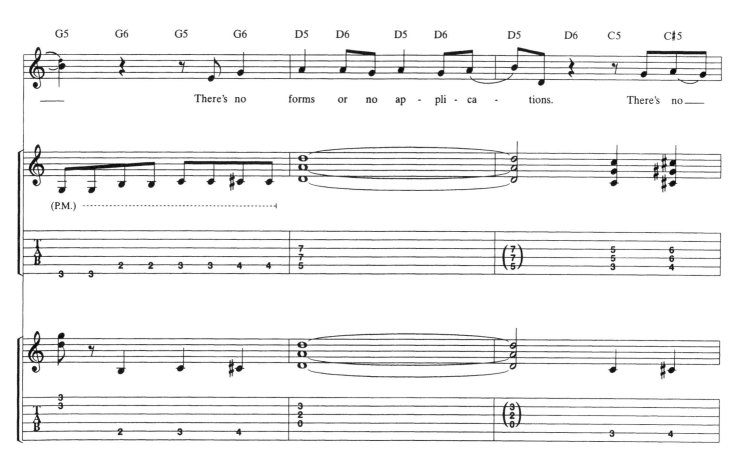

red tape ad - min - is - tra - tions. It's the A - mer - i - can Hon - ky - Tonk

Bar As - so - ci - a - tion.

D S. 𝄋 al Coda

†Doubled by Gtr. II for 2 measures.

Outro:
w/Rhy. Figs. 1 *(Gtrs. I & III)* **and 1A** *(Gtr. II) (2 times)*

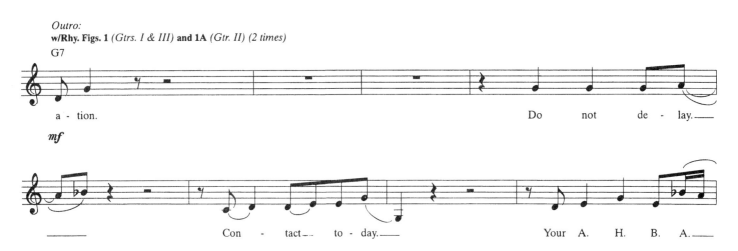

Your A. H. B. A.

Feedback

Verse 2:
When Uncle Sam dips into your pocket
For most things you don't mind.
But when your dollar goes to all of those
Standing in a welfare line.
Rejoice you have voice
If you're concerned about the destination
Of this great nation.
It's called the American Honky-Tonk Bar Association.
(To Chorus:)

THE BEACHES OF CHEYENNE

Words and Music by
DAN ROBERTS, BRYAN KENNEDY
and GARTH BROOKS

The Beaches of Cheyenne - 4 - 2
28975

Chorus:

41

Verse 2:
Well, he was up in Wyoming,
And drew a bull no man could ride.
He promised her he'd turn out;
Well, it turned out that he lied.
And all the dreams that they'd been living
In the California sand,
Died right there beside him in Cheyenne.
(To Chorus:)

Verse 3:
They never found her body,
Just her diary by the bed.
It told about the fight they had,
And the words that she had said.
When he told her he was ridin',
She said, "Then I don't give a damn
If you never come back from Cheyenne."
(To Chorus:)

The Beaches of Cheyenne - 4 - 4
28975

BEER RUN

Words and Music by
KIM WILLIAMS, AMANDA WILLIAMS,
KEITH ANDERSON, GEORGE DUCAS
and KENT BLAZY

Beer Run - 6 - 1
28975

44

46

Outro:

Repeat ad lib. and fade

Verse 2:
My buddies and their babies letting down their hair,
As long as we're together, it don't matter where.
Ain't got a lot of money but we just don't care,
Knowing half the fun is in the getting there.
Aztec, long necks, paychecks spent.
Oh, it's a B double E double R.U.N.
(To Bridge:)

Verse 3:
Laughing and bragging and a-carrying on,
We loaded up the wagons and we headed home.
I guess half a dozen cases doesn't last that long,
Come tomorrow morning, it'll all be gone.
Then, it's turn around, leave town.
Sounds again like a B double E double R.U.N.
(To Coda)

THE CHANGE

Words and Music by
TONY ARATA and WAYNE TESTER

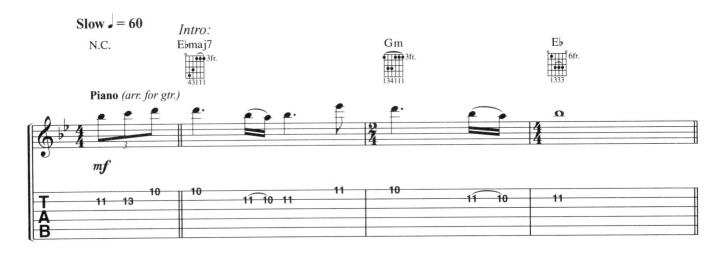

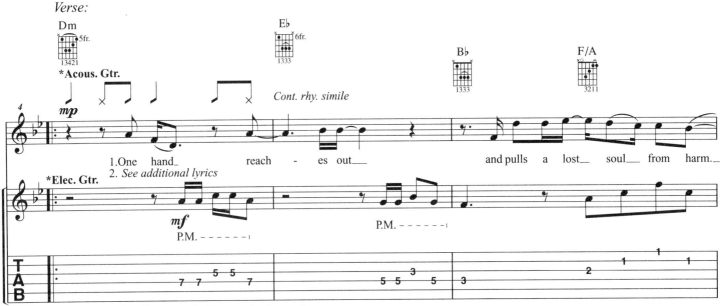

*Acous. & Elec. Gtrs. tacet 1st 8 meas., 1st time only.

The Change - 4 - 1
28975

50

The Change - 4 - 3
28975

Verse 2:
This heart still believes
That love and mercy still exist.
While all the hatreds rage and
So many say that love is all but pointless
In madness such as this.
Itís like trying to stop a fire
With the moisture from a kiss.
(To Chorus:)

THE DANCE

Words and Music by
TONY ARATA

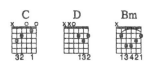

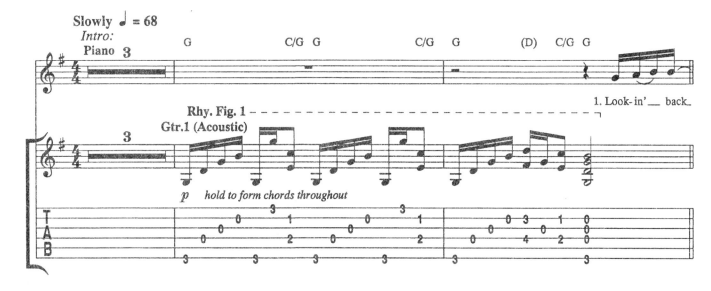

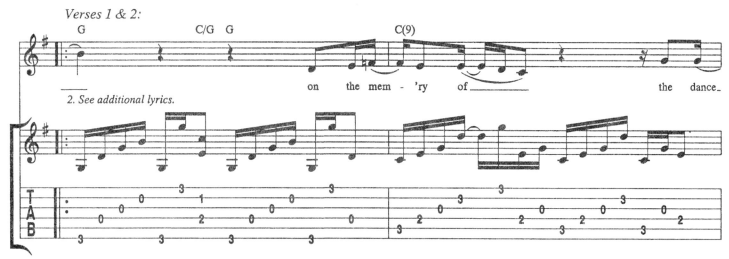

The Dance - 6 - 1
28975

Chorus:

* Gtr. 1 cont. sim. finger picking, see chord diagrams
+ Fade in w/vol. knob

The Dance - 6 - 2
28975

Rhy. Fill 1
Gtr.1

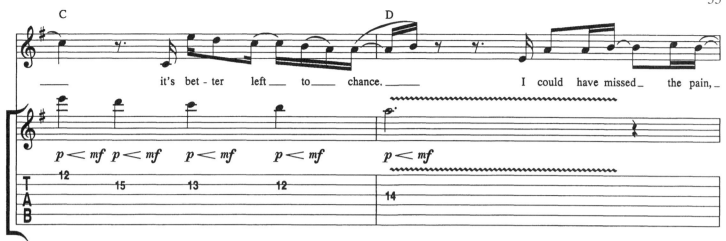

it's bet - ter left ___ to ___ chance. ___ I could have missed_ the pain,

but I'd of had ___ to ___ miss ___ the ___ dance.

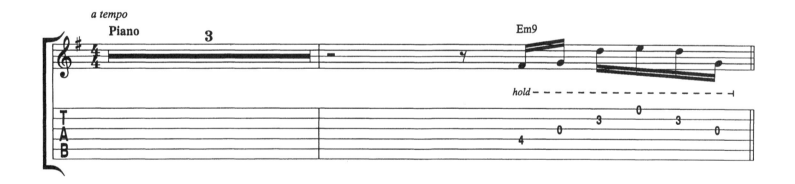

56

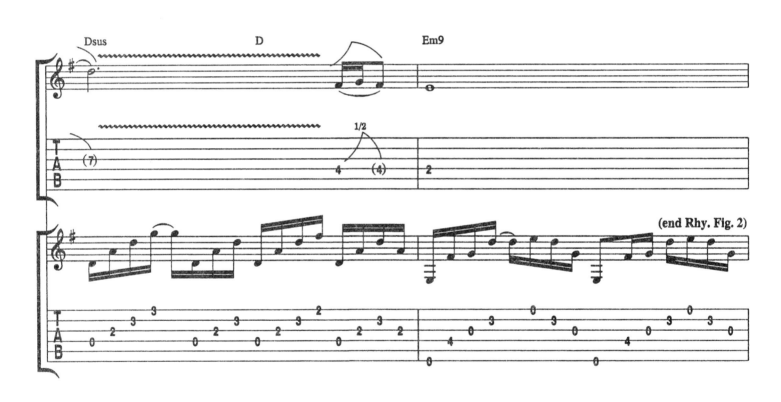

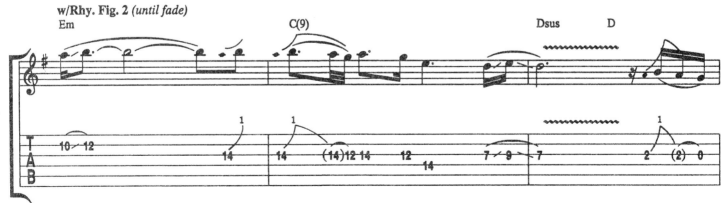

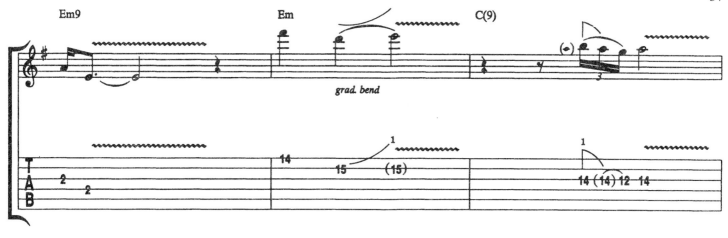

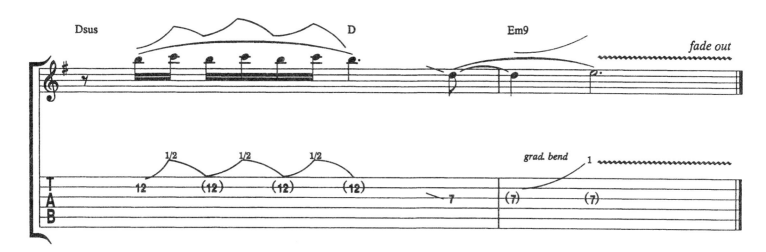

Verse 2:

Holding you, I held everything.
For a moment, wasn't I a king?
If I'd only known how the king would fall.
Hey, who's to say?
You know I might have changed it all.

(To Chorus:)

THE FEVER

Words and Music by
STEVEN TYLER, JOE PERRY,
BRYCE KENNEDY and DAN ROBERTS

rat - tle - snake   bite.____
lec - tric   chair.____
We're all   here____ 'cause he's   not all   there____ to night.____

62

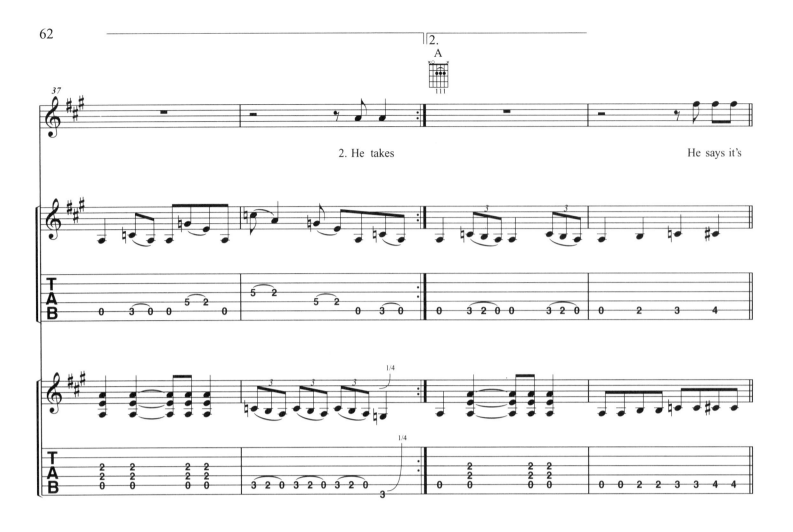

The Fever - 9 - 5
28975

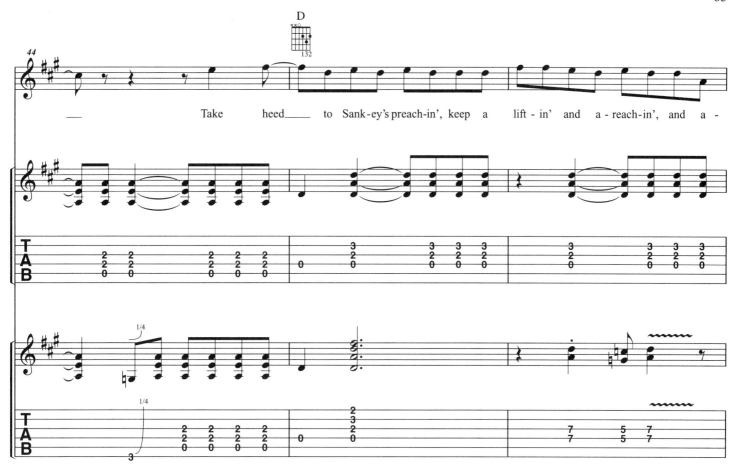

Take heed___ to Sank-ey's preach-in', keep a lift-in' and a-reach-in', and a-

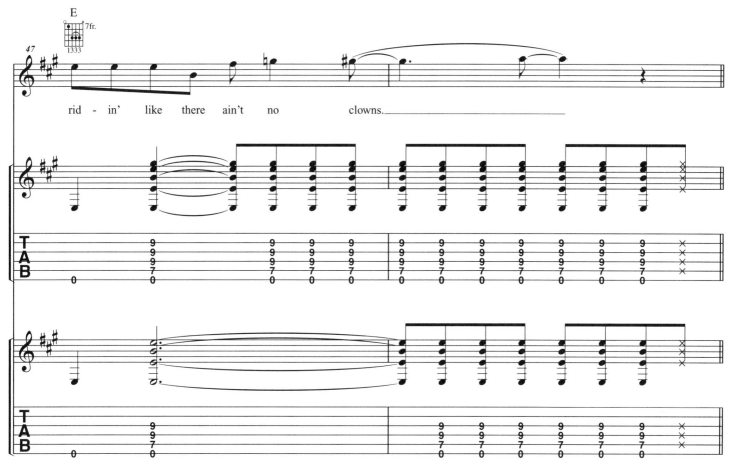

rid-in' like there ain't no clowns._____

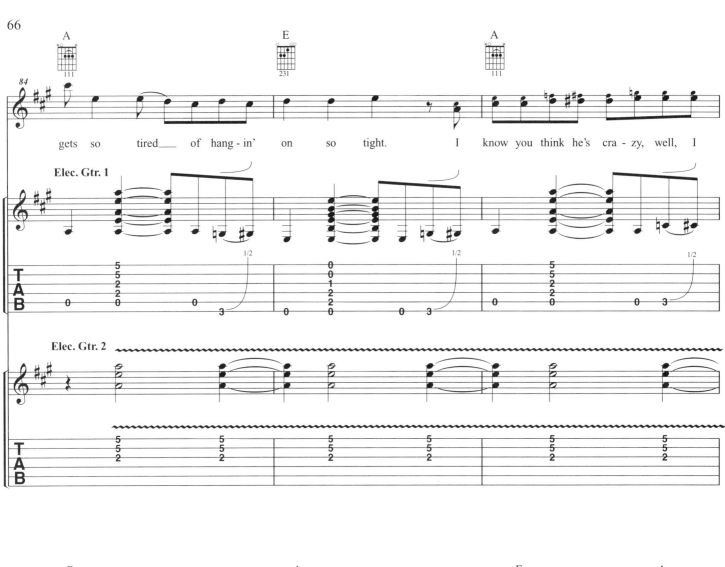

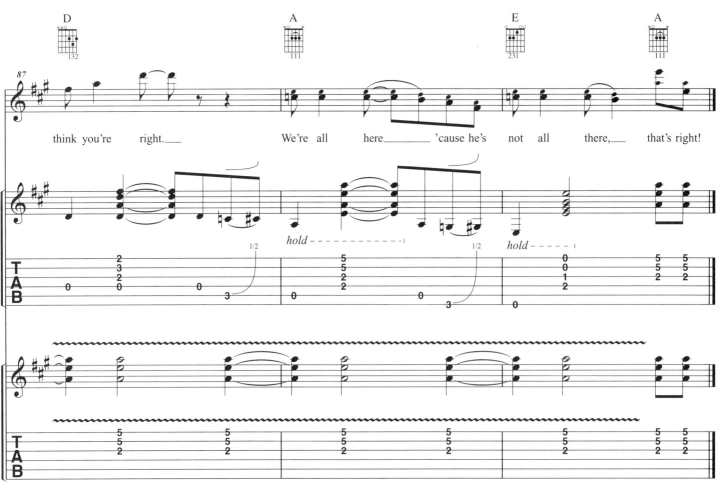

FRIENDS IN LOW PLACES

Words and Music by
DEWAYNE BLACKWELL
and EARL BUD LEE

Moderate country rock ♩ = 100

Intro:

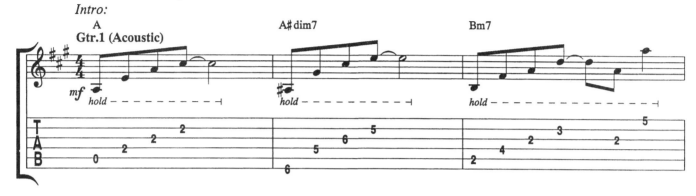

𝄋 *Verses 1 & 2:*

1. Blame it all on my roots, ___ I showed up in boots ___ and
2. *See additional lyrics.*

ru-ined your black ___ tie af-fair. ___ The last one to know, ___ the

Friends in Low Places - 9 - 1
28975

68

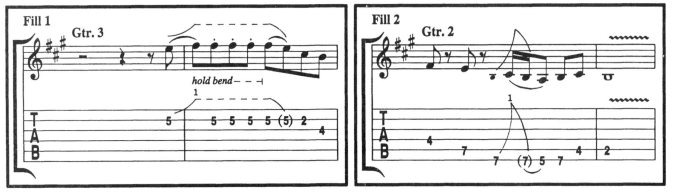

72

Chorus:
w/Rhy. Figs. 1 & 1a

I've got friends __ in low plac - es where the whis-key __ drowns, __ and the

beer __ chas - es my blues __ a - way. __ And I'll be o - kay. __

w/Rhy. Figs. 2 & 2a

Yeah, I'm not big __ on so - cial grac - es. Think I'll slip on __ down __ to the

o - a - sis. Oh, __ I've got friends __ in low __ plac -

- es. __ I've __

Gtr. 3

w/Rhy. Figs. 1 & 1a

__ got friends __ in low plac - es where the whis-key __ drowns __ and the

fdbk
(8va)

fdbk
(8va)

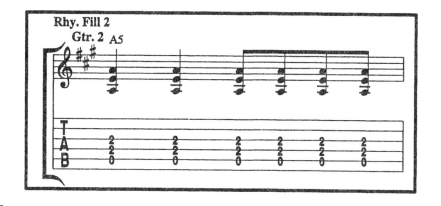

74

Verse 2:

Well, I guess I was wrong.
I just don't belong.
But then, I've been there before.
Everything's all right.
I'll just say goodnight,
And I'll show myself to the door.
Hey, I didn't mean
To cause a big scene.
Just give me an hour and then,
Well, I'll be as high
As that ivory tower
That you're livin' in.
(To Chorus:)

GOOD RIDE COWBOY

Words and Music by
BRYAN KENNEDY, JERROD LEE NIEMANN,
RICHIE BROWN and BOB DOYLE

82

Good Ride Cowboy - 9 - 7
28975

IF TOMORROW NEVER COMES

Words and Music by
KENT BLAZY and
GARTH BROOKS

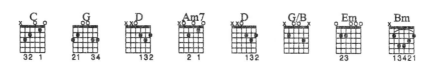

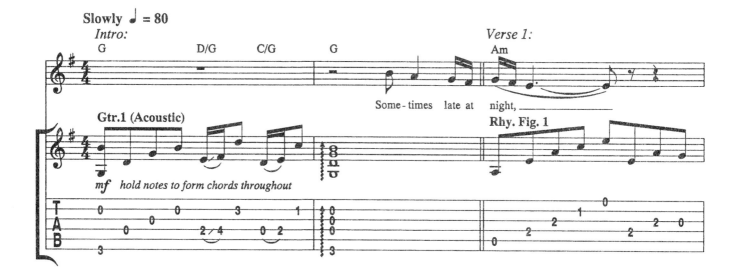

If Tomorrow Never Comes - 7 - 1
28975

86

If Tomorrow Never Comes - 7 - 2
28975

and she must face ____ this world with - out me, ____

is the love I gave ____ her in ____ the past ____ gon - na be e - nough ____ to last ____

____ if to - mor - row nev - er comes? ____

IN ANOTHER'S EYES

Words and Music by
BOBBY WOOD, JOHN PEPPARD
and GARTH BROOKS

Slowly ♩ = 72

Intro:

In Another's Eyes - 8 - 1
28975

96

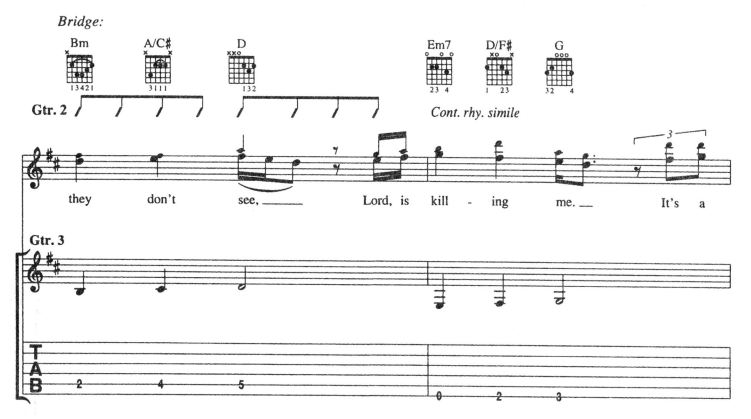

LEARNING TO LIVE AGAIN

Words and Music by
DON SCHILTZ and STEPHANIE DAVIS

Slowly ♩ = 48

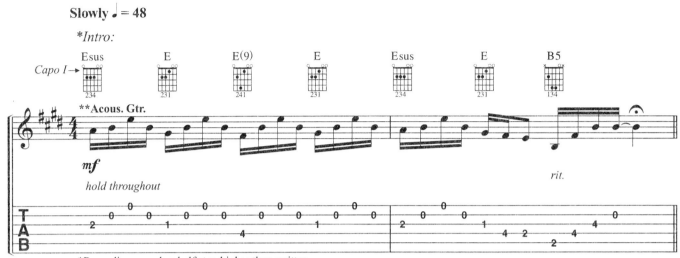

*Recording sounds a half step higher than written.
**Acous. Gtr. w/capo I. Chord frames and TAB numbers relative to capo.

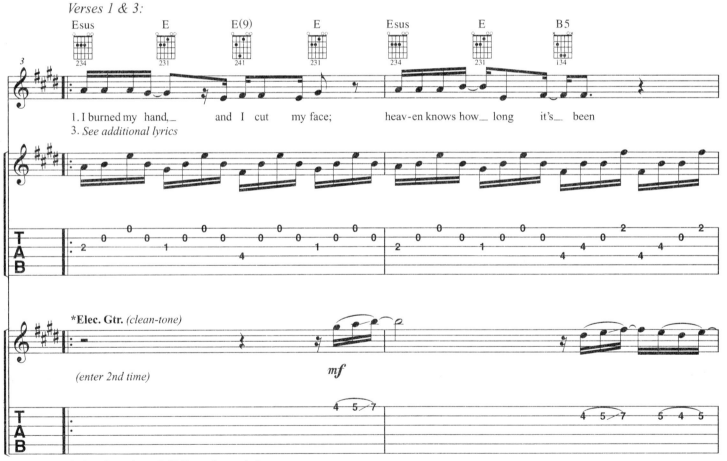

*Elec. Gtr. w/capo I. TAB numbers relative to capo.
Elec. Gtr. is a composite of Elec. Gtrs. 1 & 2.
Elec. Gtr. simile on repeats.

Learning to Live Again - 6 - 1
28975

104

D.S. 𝄋 *al Coda*

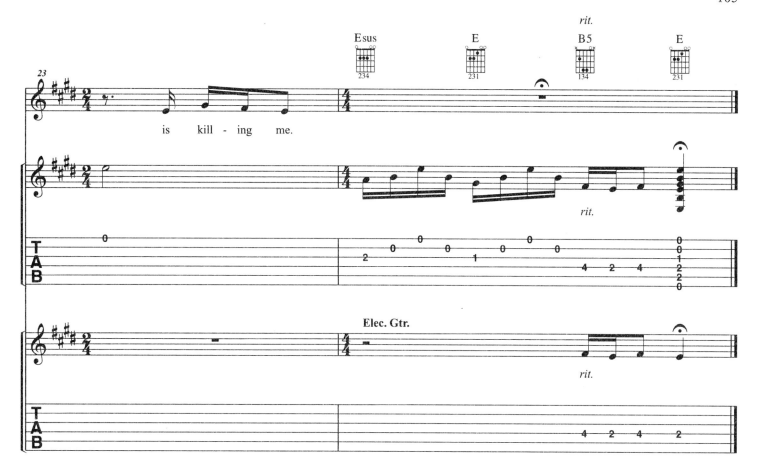

is kill - ing me.

Verse 3:
A little cafe, table for four,
But there's just conversation for three.
I like the way she let me get the door;
I wonder what she thinks of me.

Verse 4:
Debbie just whispered, "You're doing fine."
And I wish that I felt the same.
She's asked me to dance; now her hand's in mine;
Oh, my God, I've forgotten her name.
(To Chorus:)

Verse 5:
Now, here we are beneath her porch light
And I say what a great time it's been;
A kiss on the cheek, a whisper goodnight,
And I say, "Can I see you again?"

Chorus 3:
And she just smiles her best smile,
And she laughs like it's goin' out of style.
Looks into my eyes and says, "We'll see."
Oh, this learning to live again is killing me.
God, this learning to live again is killing me.

LEAVE A LIGHT ON

Words and Music by
RANDY GOODRUM and TOMMY SIMMS

Slow ballad ♩ = 66

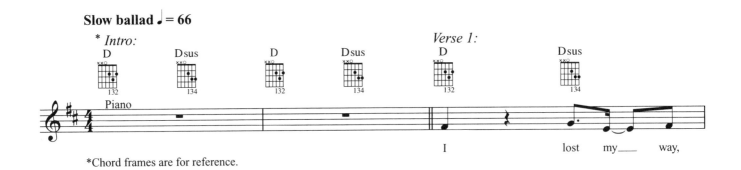

*Chord frames are for reference.

I   lost my___ way,

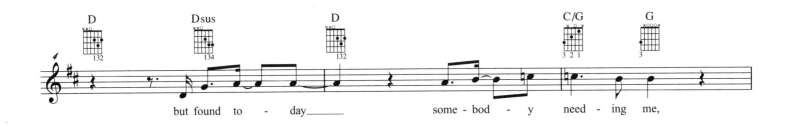

but found to - day___   some - bod - y need - ing me,

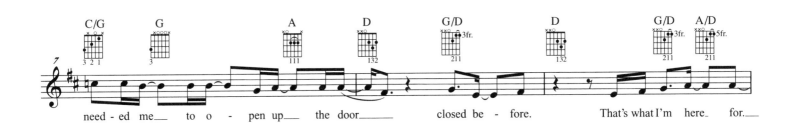

need - ed me___ to o - pen up___ the door___   closed be - fore.   That's what I'm here_ for.

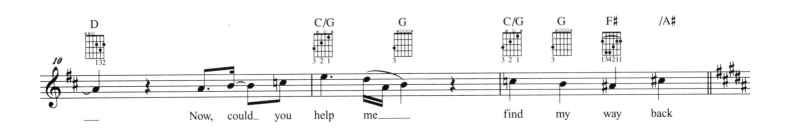

___   Now, could_ you help me___   find my way back

Chorus:

So leave a light on.___ Leave a light on___ for me_____ and I will

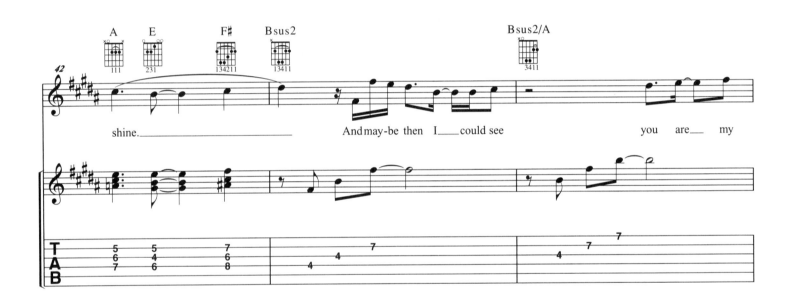

shine._____ And may-be then I___ could see   you are___ my

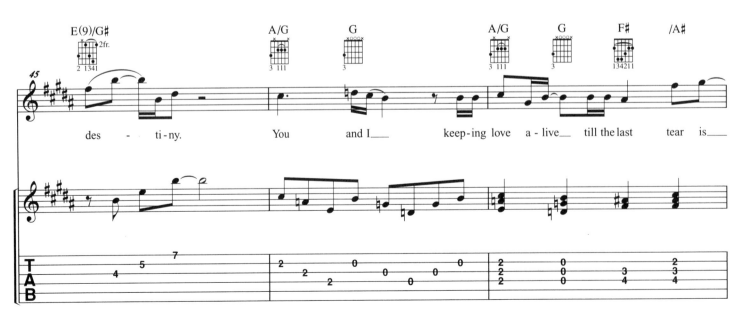

des - ti-ny.   You   and I___   keep-ing love a-live___ till the last   tear is___

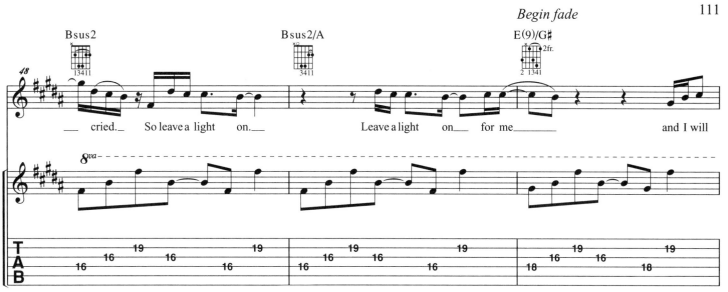

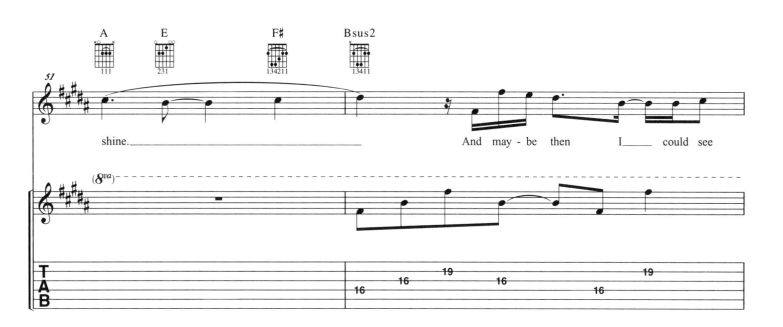

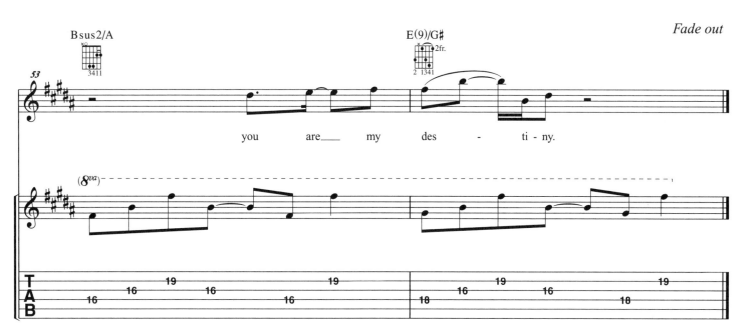

LONGNECK BOTTLE

Words and Music by
STEVE WARINER and RICK CARNES

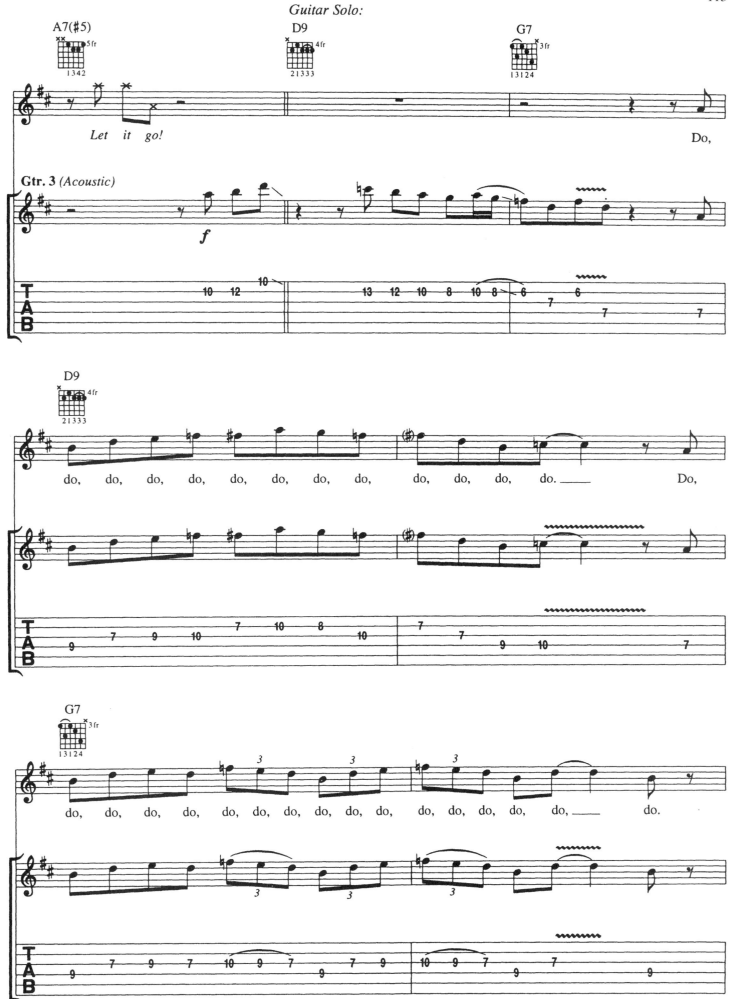

116

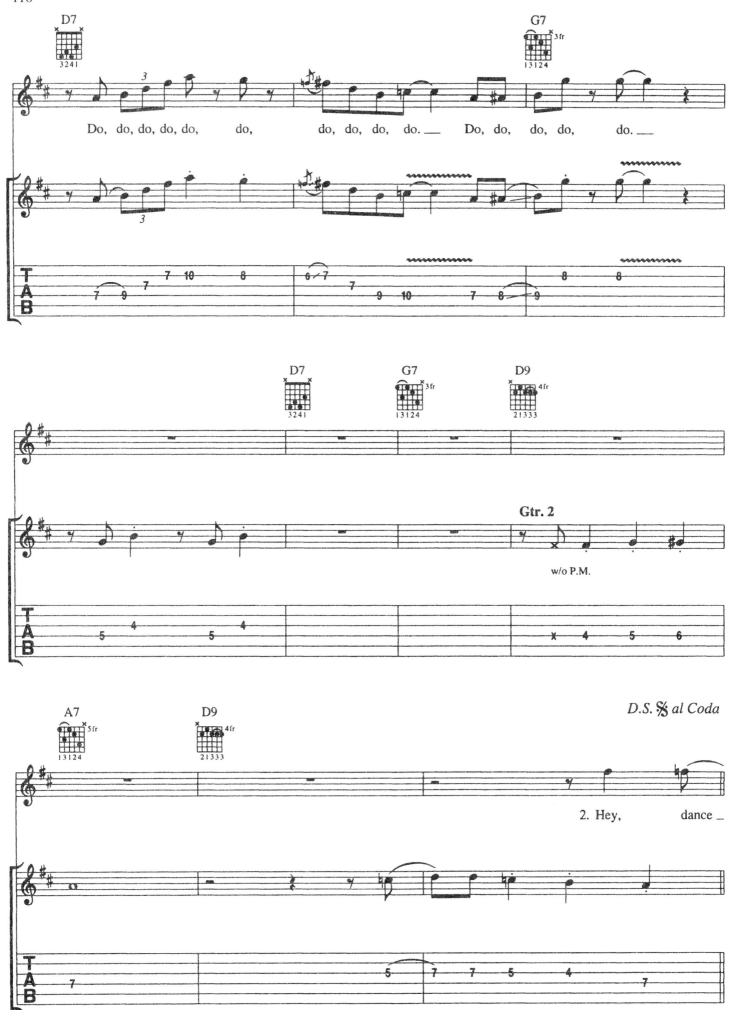

Longneck Bottle - 6 - 5
28975

MIDNIGHT SUN

Words and Music by
JERROD NIEMANN, RICHIE BROWN
and GARTH BROOKS

*Elec. Gtr. 1 w/Drop D: ⑥ = D

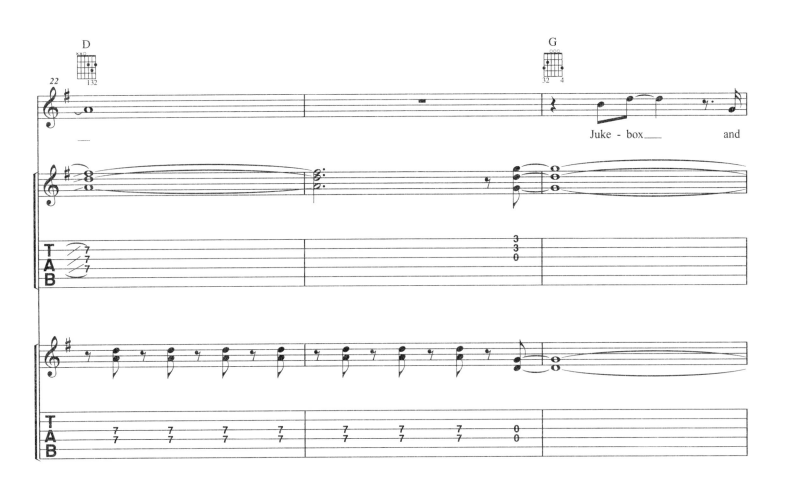

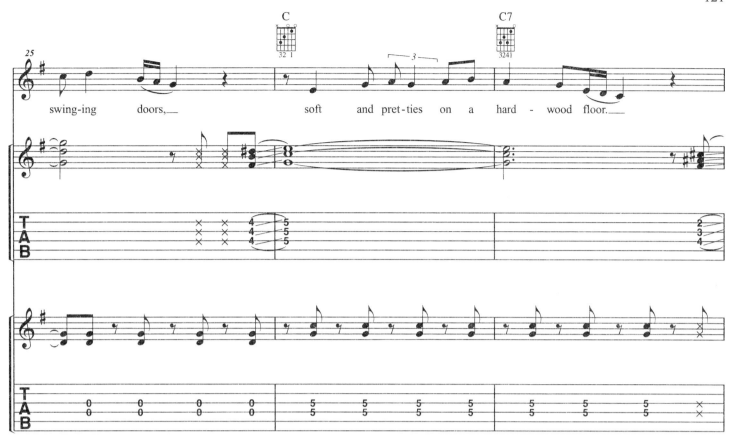

swing-ing doors,___ soft and pret-ties on a hard-wood floor.___

A cow-boy's work just___ ain't nev - er done___

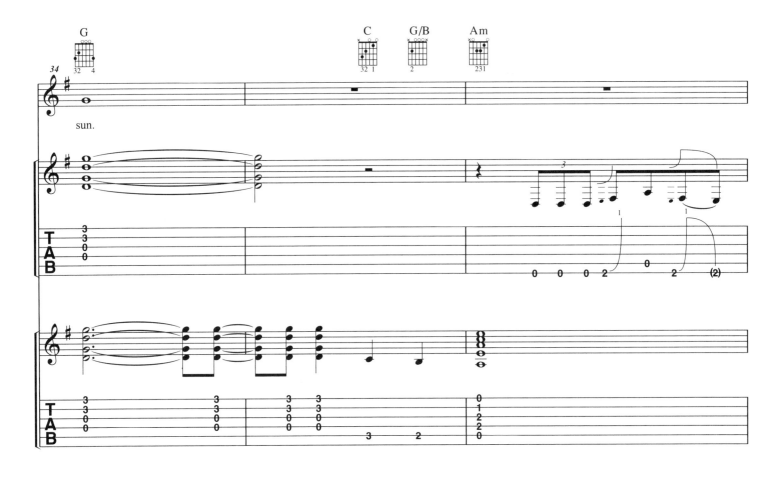

Verses 2 & 3:

2. Find a look- er, have her hold my keys,___ and tell her lat- er we'll be
3. Shoot the breeze while shoot- in' pool___ and still you're sweat- in' like a

*Acous. Gtr. resume rhy. fig. simile

*Elec. Gtrs. 1 & 2 simile 2nd time.

124

Midnight Sun - 9 - 7
28975

'Cause eight o'-clock__ comes twice a day__ and eith-er way you'll find me
Look-y there__ who waits for me, smil-in' sweet-ly, hold-in'

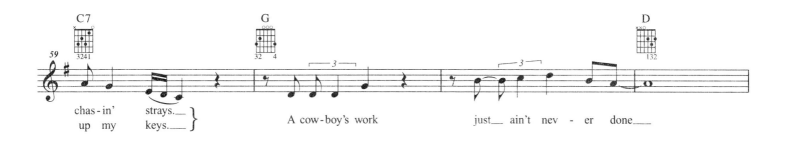

chas-in' strays.__
up my keys.__ A cow-boy's work just__ ain't nev-er done__

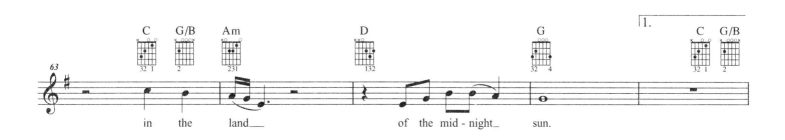

in the land__ of the mid-night__ sun.

126

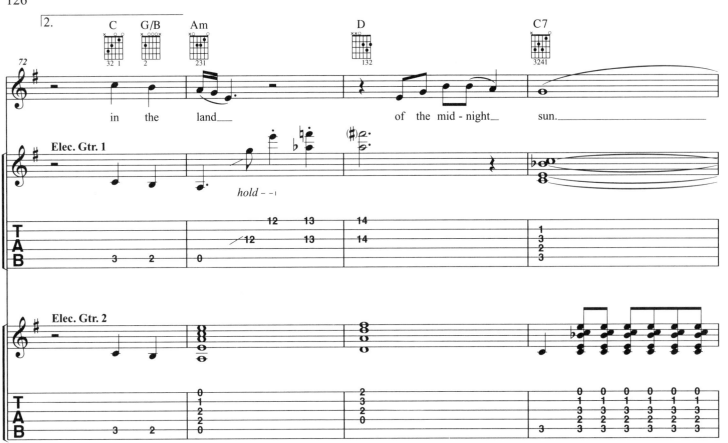

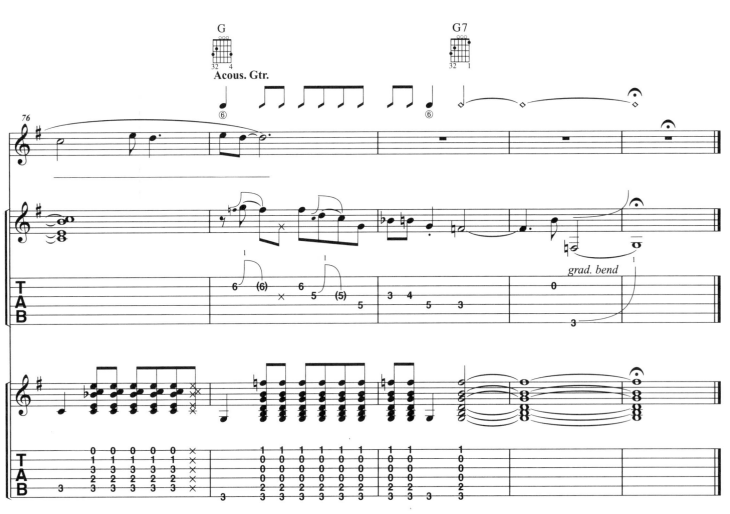

Midnight Sun - 9 - 9
28975

MUCH TOO YOUNG

Words and Music by
RANDY TAYLOR and
GARTH BROOKS

Intro:

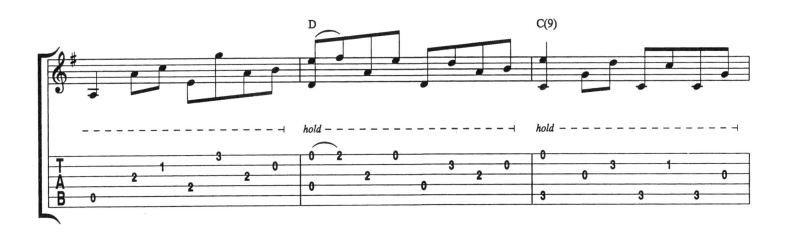

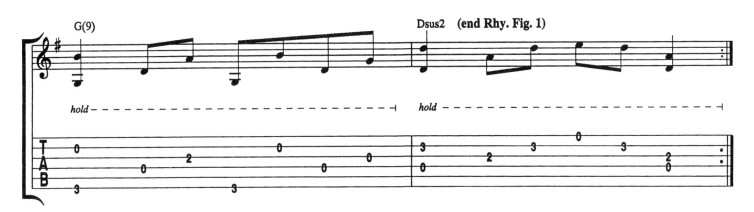

Much Too Young - 7 - 1
28975

128

Much Too Young - 7 - 3
28975

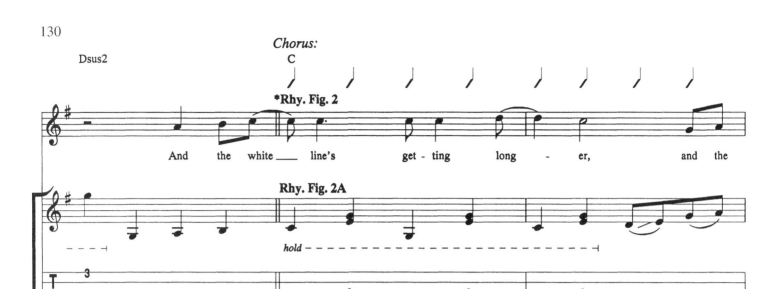

*In Rhy. Fig. 2 alternate low root, then remainder of chord, holding all notes for each chord change.

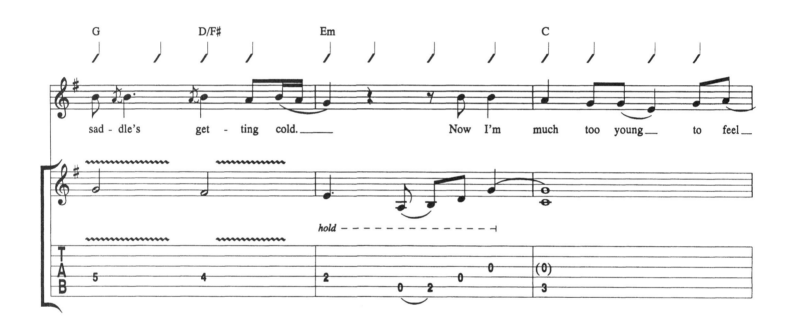

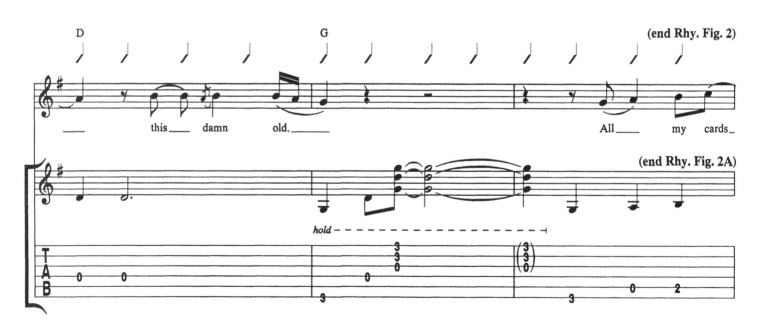

w/Rhy. Fig. 2 & 2A *(1st 6 bars only)*

are on the ta - ble, with no ace left in the hole.

Now I'm much too young to feel this damn old.

w/Rhy. Fill 1 (Gtr. 2)

Solos:
*w/Rhy. Figs. 1 & 1A *(both 2 times)*

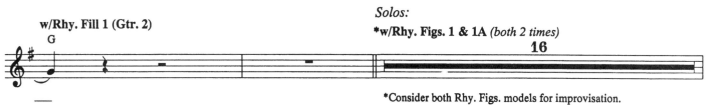

16

*Consider both Rhy. Figs. models for improvisation.

Verse 3:
w/Rhy. Fig. 1 *(2 times)*

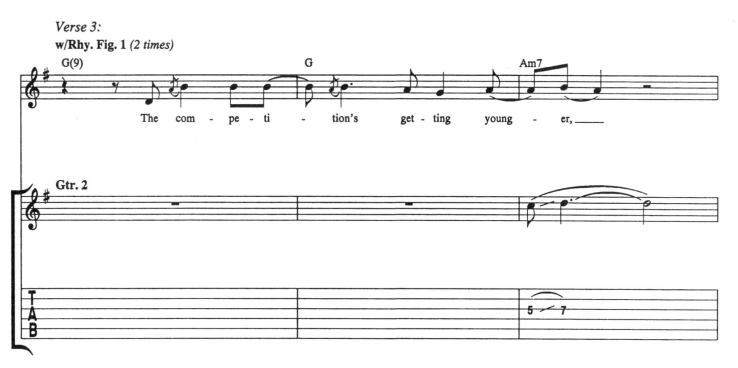

The com - pe - ti - tion's get - ting young - er,

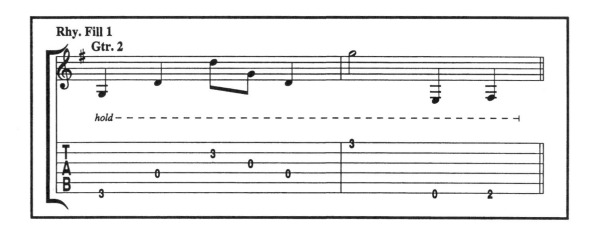

Rhy. Fill 1
Gtr. 2

hold

MORE THAN A MEMORY

Words and Music by
BILLY MONTANA, LEE BRICE
and KYLE JACOBS

*Recording sounds a half step higher than written.
**Acous. Gtr. w/capo I. Chord frames relative to capo.

More Than a Memory - 6 - 1
28975

136

*Bass plays A.

Chorus 3:

dial-in' her num-ber just to hang up the phone,_ driv - in' 'cross town just to see if she's home,_

wak-in' a friend_ in the dead of night_ just_ to hear him say, "It's gon - na be al - right."_ When you're find-

Resume rhy. fig. simile

- in' things to do not to fall_ a - sleep,_ 'cause you know_ she's wait-ing in_ your_ dreams,_

PAPA LOVED MAMA

Words and Music by
KIM WILLIAMS and GARTH BROOKS

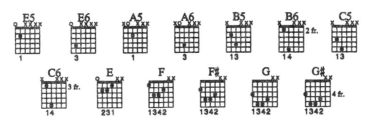

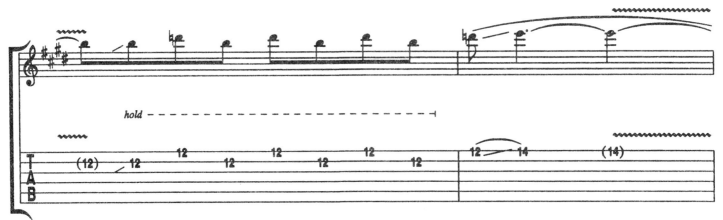

Papa Loved Mama - 10 - 1
28975

(end Rhy. Fig 1)
C5 C6 C5 C6 B5 B6 B5 B6 E5 E6 E5 E6
w/Rhy. Fig. 1 (1st 7 bars only)
(end P.M.)
need-ed more to hold than just a tel - e - phone. Pa - pa called Ma-ma each and
Gtr. 3 Rhy. Fig. 2
mf
P.M. (until change)
E5 E6 E5 E6 A5 A6 A5 A6 A5 A6 A5 A6
ev - 'ry night, just to ask her how she was, and if us kids were al - right. Ma -
B5 B6 B5 B6 B5 B6 B5 B6 C5 C6 C5 C6
- ma would wait for that call to come in, but when Dad - dy'd hang up, she was
B5 B6 E5 E6 E5 E6
gone a - gain. Ma -
(end Rhy. Fig. 2)
1/4
(end P.M.)

146

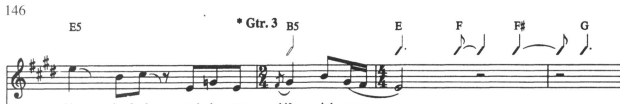

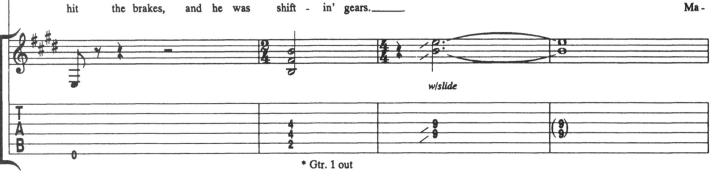

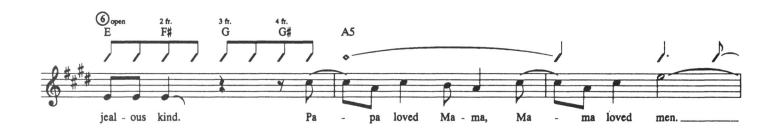

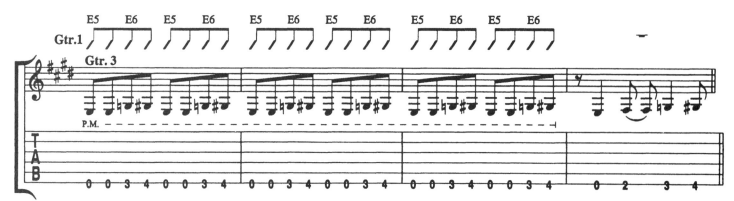

Papa Loved Mama - 10 - 7
28975

Papa Loved Mama - 10 - 8
28975

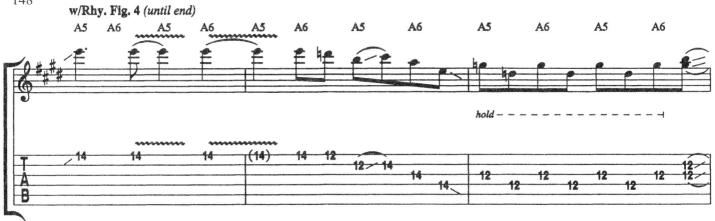

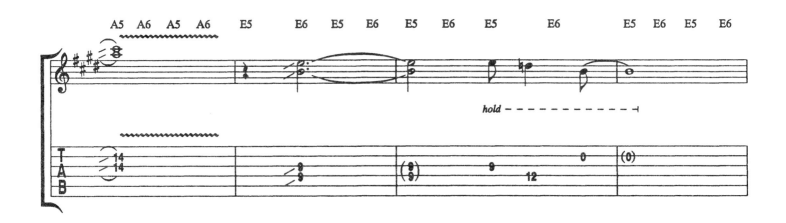

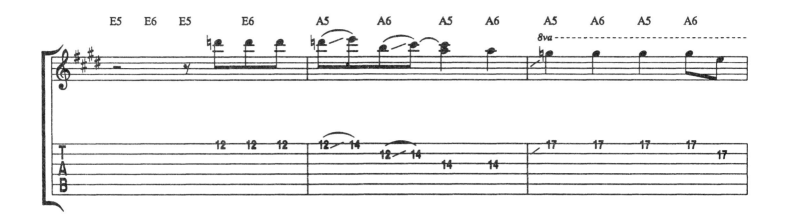

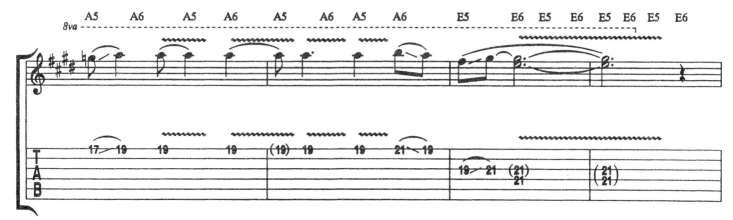

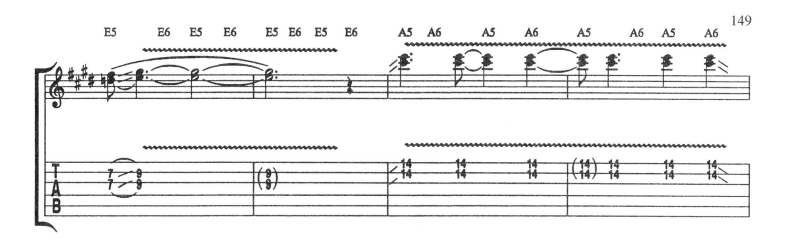

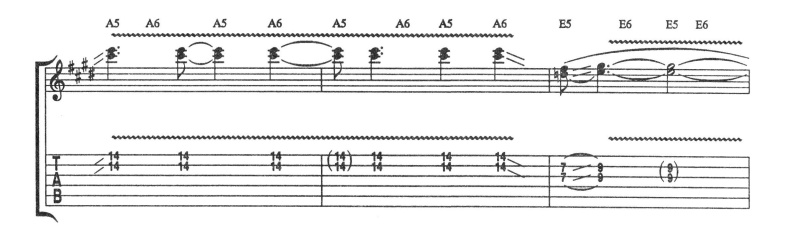

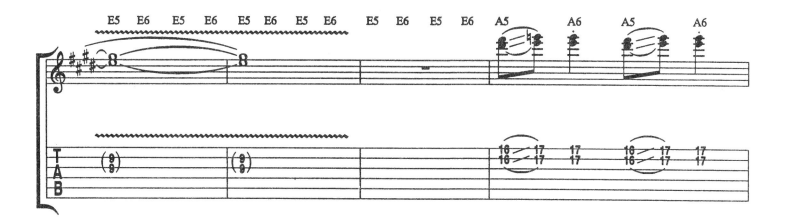

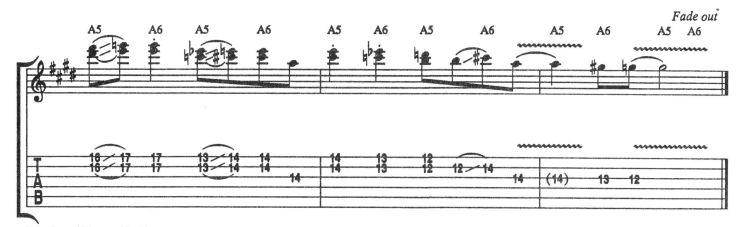

Papa Loved Mama - 10 - 10
28975

THE RIVER

Words and Music by
VICTORIA SHAW and GARTH BROOKS

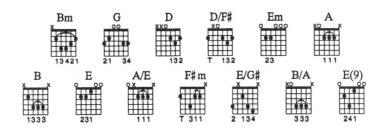

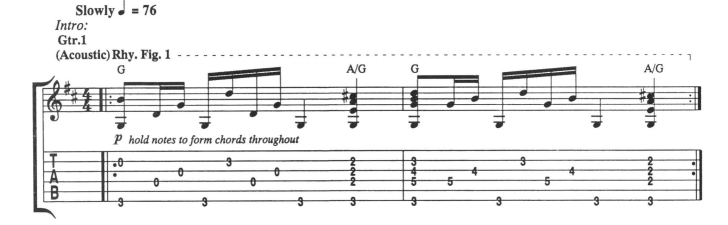

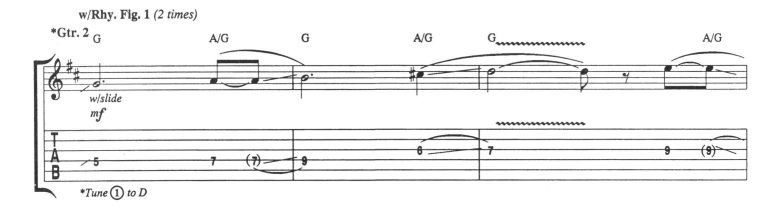

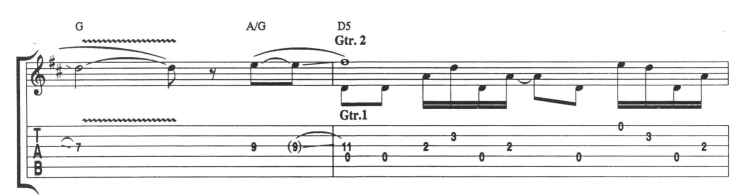

The River - 9 - 1
28975

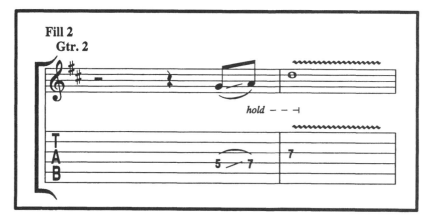

The River - 9 - 2
28975

152

154

156

The River - 9 - 7
28975

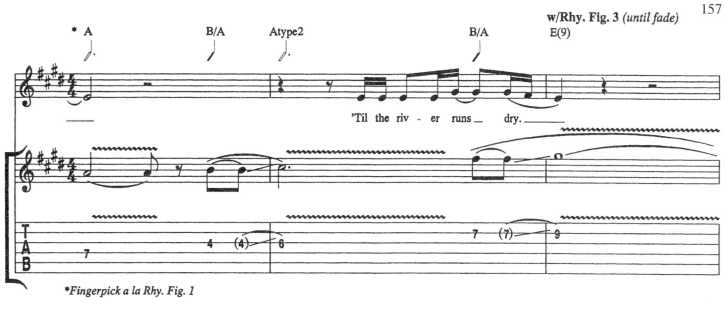

'Til the riv - er runs__ dry. ____

Fingerpick a la Rhy. Fig. 1

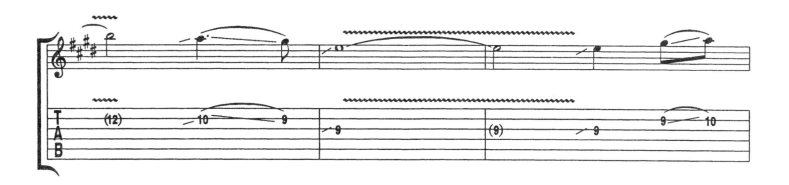

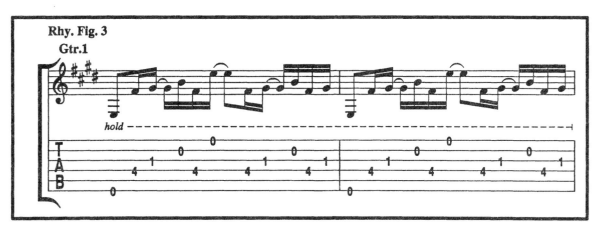

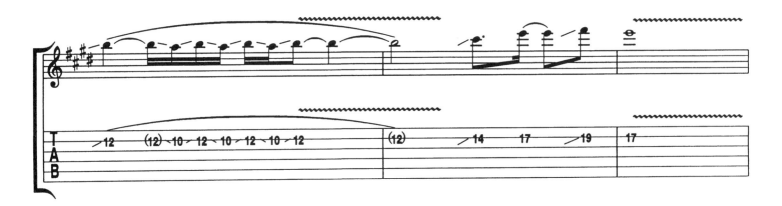

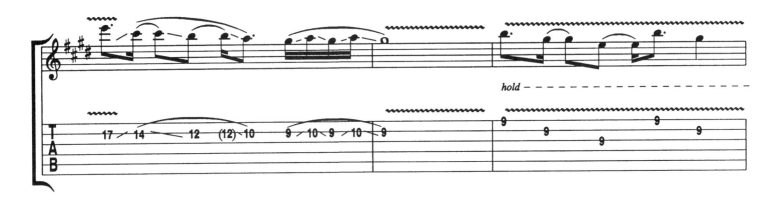

Verse 2:

Too many times we stand aside
And let the waters slip away
'Til what we put off 'til tomorrow
Has now become today.
So, don't you sit upon the shoreline
And say you're satisfied.
Choose to chance the rapids
And dare to dance the tide. Yes, I will. . .
(To Chorus:)

THAT SUMMER

Words and Music by
PAT ALGER, SANDY MAHL
and GARTH BROOKS

160

That Summer - 9 - 2
28975

There was a dif-f'rence in her laugh-ter.___ There was a soft-ness in her eyes.___

And on___ the air___ there was___ a hun-ger___

ev-en a boy could re-cog-nize. She had a need to feel the thun-der,___

to chase the light-nin' from the skies.___

164

There's nev-er been an-oth-er sum-mer_____ when I___ have ev-er learned so

much.

We had a need to feel the

night

*Gtr. 3

*Tune down ⑥ to D.

Guitar Solo:

P.M. ---------

That Summer - 9 - 6
28975

That Summer - 9 - 7
28975

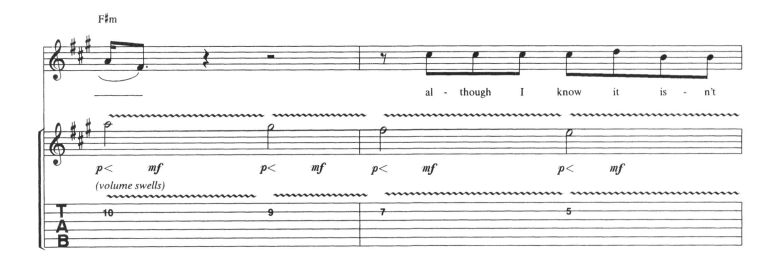

RODEO

Words and Music by
RANDY TAYLOR and GARTH BROOKS

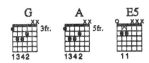

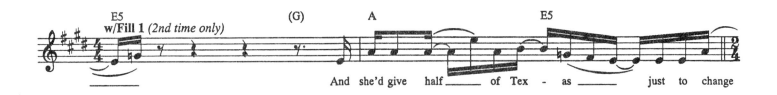

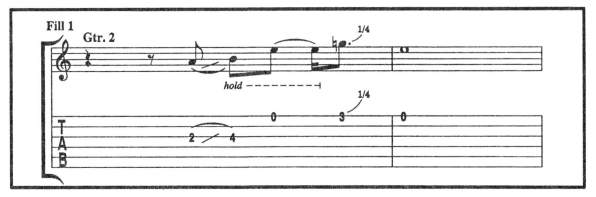

Rodeo - 6 - 1
28975

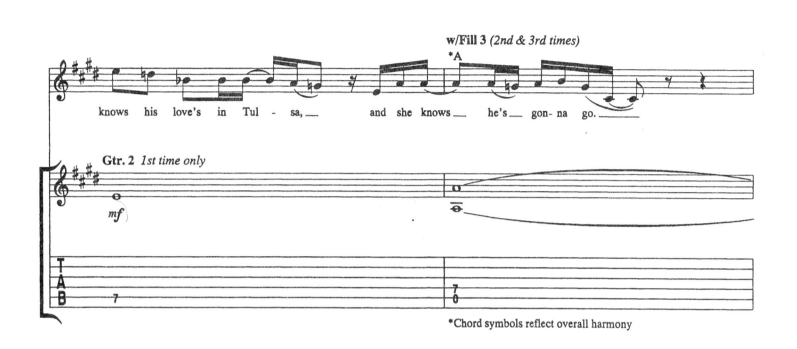

*Chord symbols reflect overall harmony

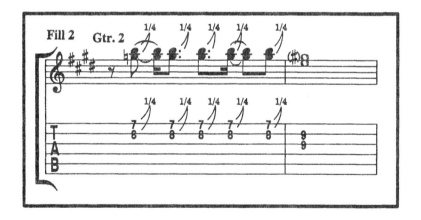

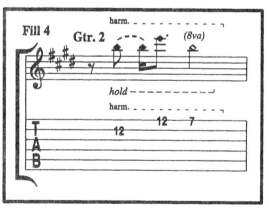

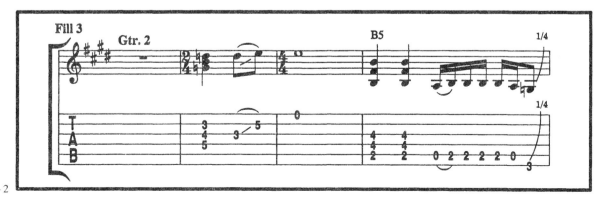

Rodeo - 6 - 2
28975

170

Rodeo - 6 - 3
28975

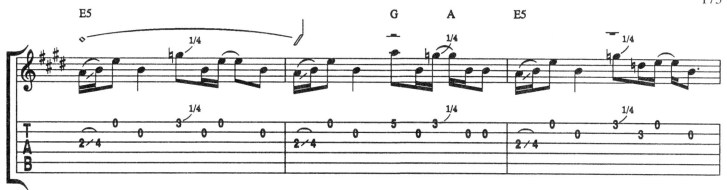

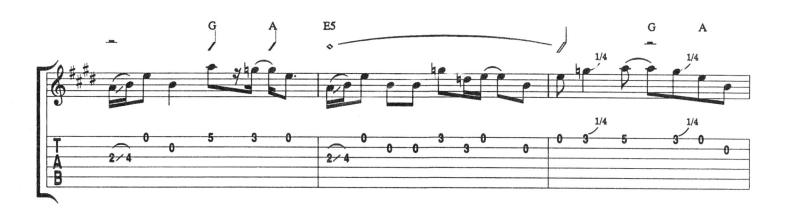

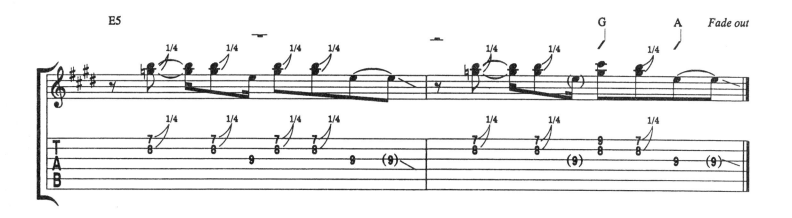

Verse 2:

She does her best to hold him
When his love comes to call.
But his need for it controls him
And her back's against the wall.
And it's "So long, girl, I'll see you.",
When it's time for him to go.
You know the woman wants her cowboy
Like he wants his rodeo.

(To Chorus:)

Verse 3:

It'll drive a cowboy crazy.
It'll drive the man insane.
And he'll sell off everything he owns
Just to pay to play her game.
And a broken home and some broken bones
Is all he'll have to show
For all the years that he spent chasin'
This dream they call rodeo.

(To Chorus:)

SHAMELESS

Words and Music by
BILLY JOEL

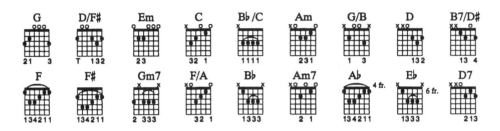

Moderate rock ♩ = 72

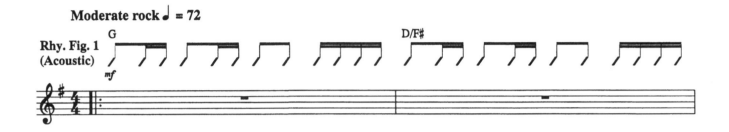

1. Well, I'm

Verses 1 & 2:

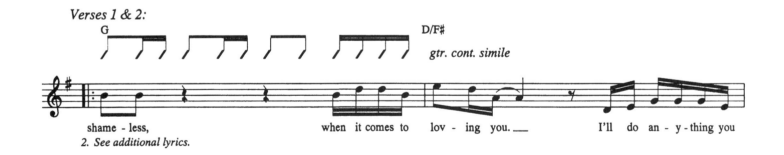

shame - less,
2. See additional lyrics.

when it comes to lov - ing you.___ I'll do an - y - thing you

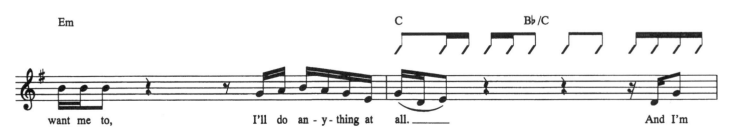

want me to, I'll do an - y - thing at all._____ And I'm

Shameless - 8 - 1
28975

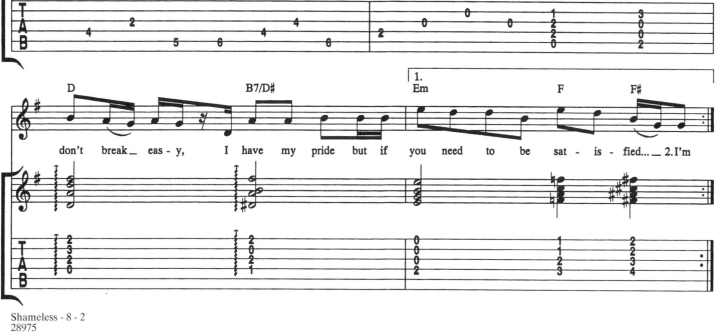

176

your world now, I can't re-fuse, ___ I've nev-er had so much to lose. ___

Guitar Solo:
w/Rhy. Fig. 1

Oh, I'm shame - less! ___

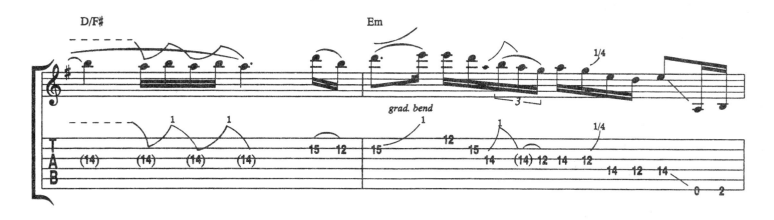

w/Rhy. Fig. 1 *(1st 3 bars only)*

Shameless - 8 - 4
28975

180

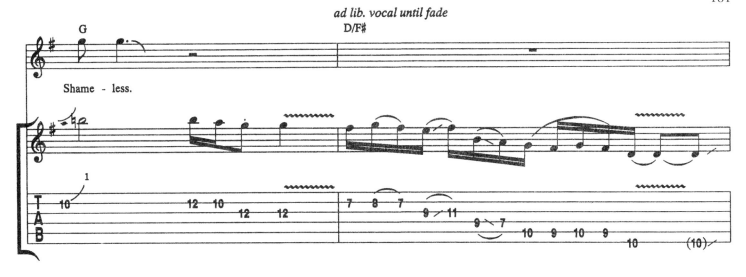

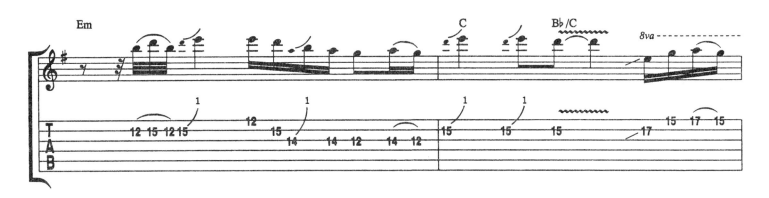

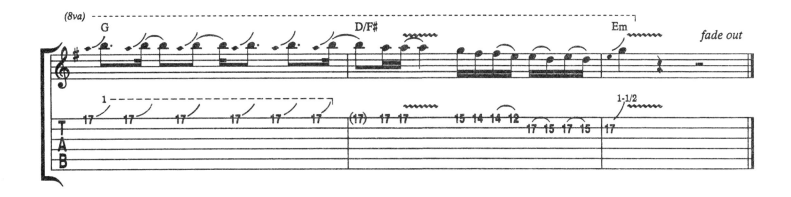

Verse 2:

I'm shameless, oh honey, I don't have a prayer.
Every time I see you standing there,
I go down upon my knees.
And I'm changing, swore I'd never compromise.
Oh, but you convinced me otherwise.
I'll do anything you please.
You see, in all my life I've never found
What I couldn't resist, what I couldn't turn down.
I could walk away from anyone I ever knew,
But I can't walk away from you.
(To Bridge:)

STANDING OUTSIDE THE FIRE

Words and Music by
JENNY YATES
and GARTH BROOKS

*Two acoustic guitars arranged for one guitar.

1. We call them cool.___ Those hearts that have no scars___ to show.___
2. *See additional lyrics*

The ones that nev-er do___ let go,_____ and risk the

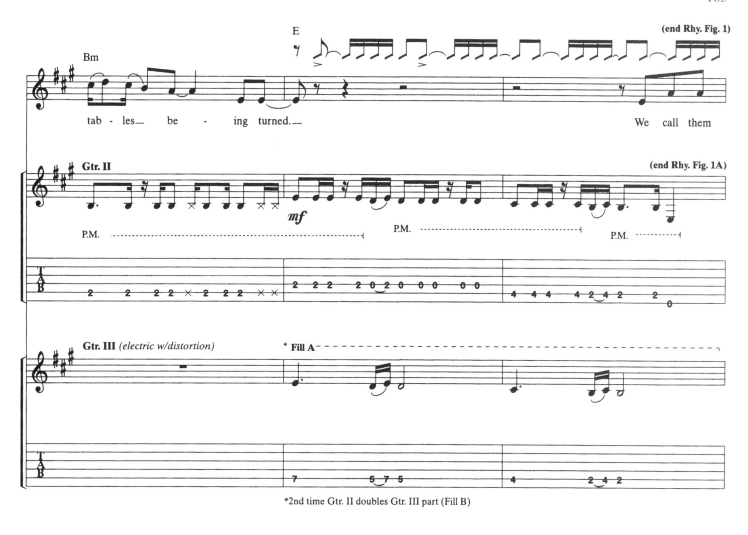

*2nd time Gtr. II doubles Gtr. III part (Fill B)

Verse 2:
We call them strong.
Those who can face this world alone.
Who seem to get by on their own.
Those who will never take the fall.

We call them weak,
Who are unable to resist
The slightest chance love might exist,
And for that forsake it all.

Bridge 2:
They're so hell bent on giving, walking a wire.
Convinced it's not living if you stand outside the fire.
(To Chorus:)

THE THUNDER ROLLS

Words and Music by
PAT ALGER and GARTH BROOKS

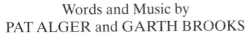

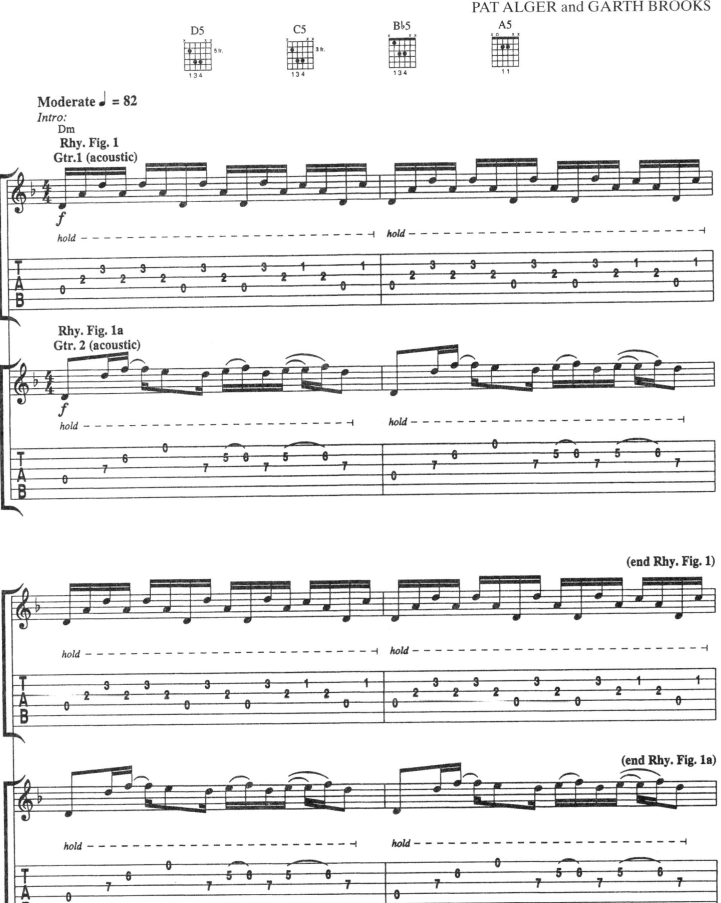

Verse 1:

1. Three-thir-ty in the morn-ing, not a soul in sight,_ the cit-y's look-in' like a ghost town on a

moon-less sum-mer night._ Rain-drops on a wind-shield, there's a

Rhy. Fig. 2

Rhy. Fig. 2a

(end Rhy. Fig. 2)

(end Rhy. Fig. 2a)

The Thunder Rolls - 10 - 2
28975

192

The Thunder Rolls - 10 - 5
28975

195

The Thunder Rolls - 10 - 8
28975

196

The Thunder Rolls - 10 - 9
28975

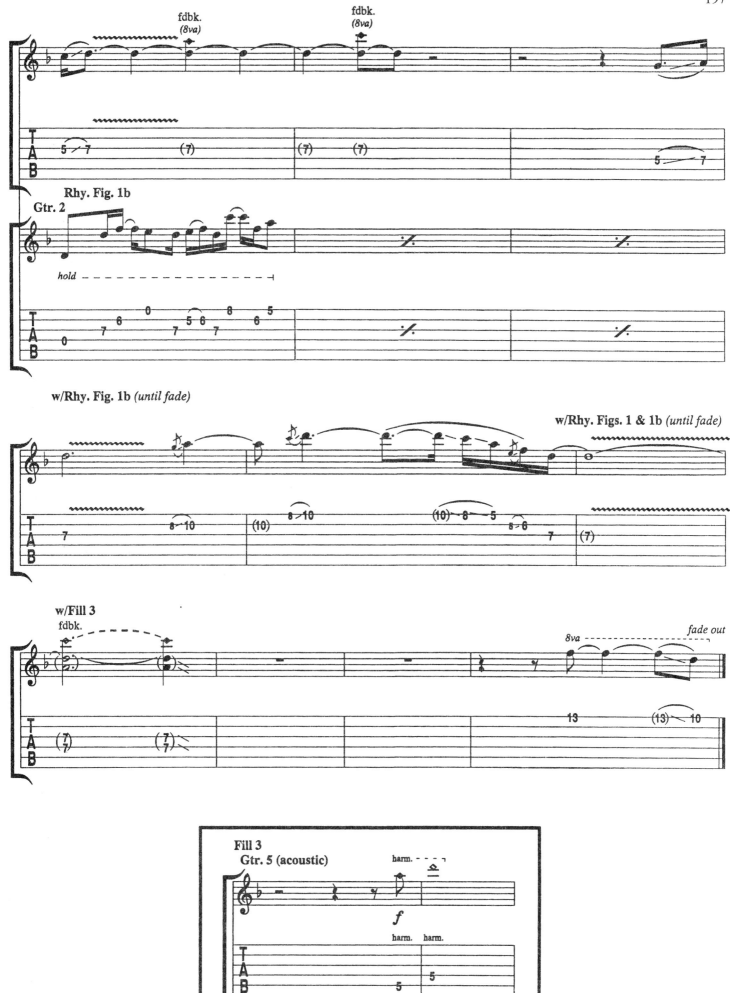

TO MAKE YOU FEEL MY LOVE

Words and Music by
BOB DYLAN

TWO OF A KIND, WORKIN' ON A FULL HOUSE

Words and Music by
BOBBY BOYD,
WARREN DALE HAYNES
and *DENNIS ROBBINS*

1. Yeah, she's ___ my la - dy luck, hey I'm her wild card man. ___ To -

2. *See additional lyrics.*

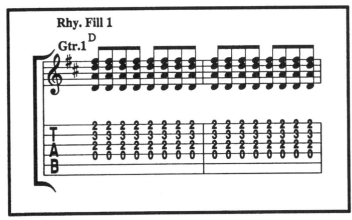

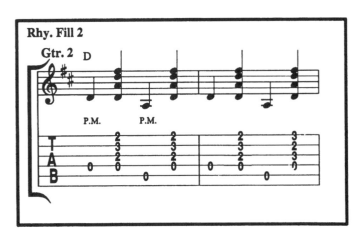

Two of a Kind, Workin' on a Full House - 5 - 1
28975

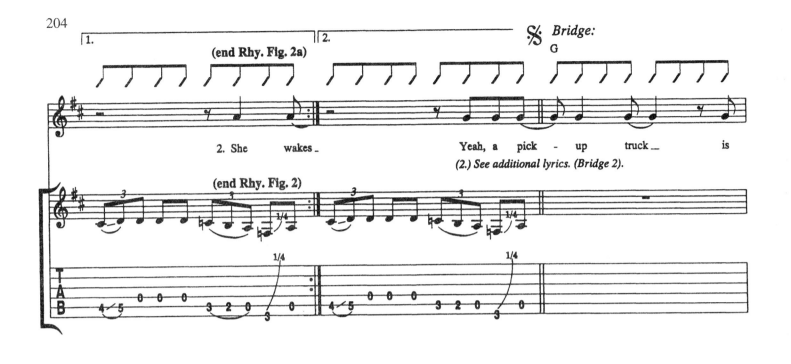

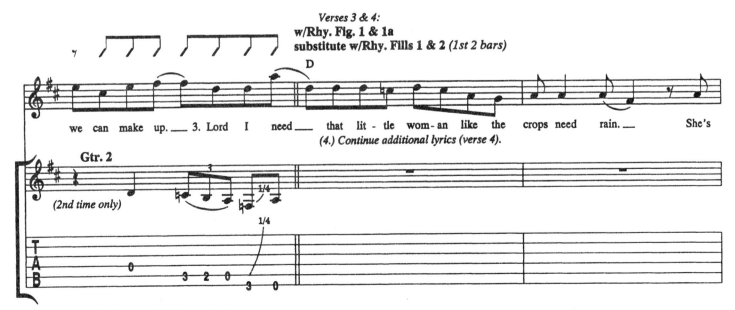

my hon - ey - comb and I'm her _____ sug - ar cane._ We real - ly fit to - geth - er if you

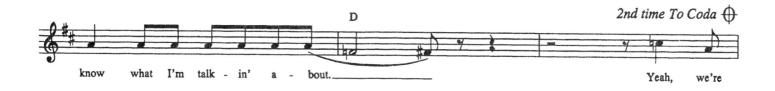

know what I'm talk - in' a - bout._____ Yeah, we're

2nd time To Coda

w/Rhy. Figs. 2 & 2a
A7

substitute w/Rhy. Fill 4 (Gtr.2)
D

two of a kind, ___ work - in' on ___ a full house.

w/Rhy. Figs. 2 & 2a
A7

substitute w/Rhy. Fill 4 (Gtr.2)
D

D.S. al Coda

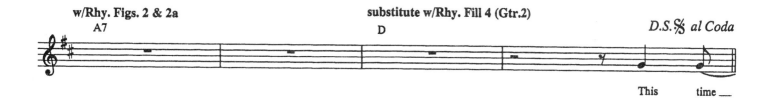

This time ___

Rhy. Fill 4

Gtr. 2 D

P.M.   P.M.   P.M. - - - - - - - - - - - - -

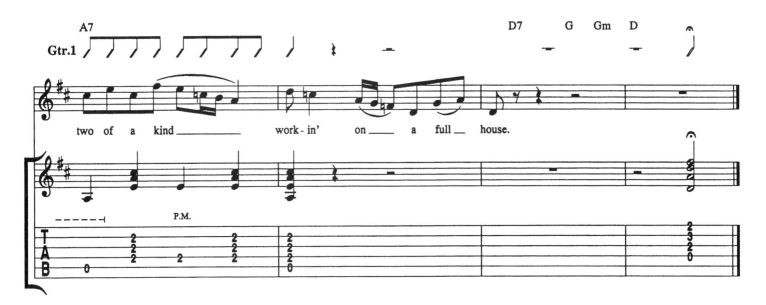

Verse 2:

She wakes me every mornin'
With a smile and a kiss.
Her strong country lovin' is hard to resist.
She's my easy lovin' woman,
I'm her hard - workin' man, no doubt.
Yeah, we're two of a kind,
Workin' on a full house.

Bridge 2:

This time I found a keeper, I made up my mind.
Lord, the perfect combination is her heart and mine.
The sky's the limit, no hill is too steep.
We're playin' for fun, but we're playin' for keeps.

Verse 4:

So draw the curtain, honey,
Turn the lights down low.
We'll find some country music on the radio.
I'm yours and you're mine.
Hey, that's what it's all about.
Yeah, we're two of a kind,
Workin' on a full house.
Lordy mama, we'll be two of a kind,
Workin' on a full house.

TWO PIÑA COLADAS

Words and Music by
SHAWN CAMP, BENITA HILL
and SANDY MASON

Moderately (Calypso feel) ♩ = 120

Intro:

N.C.

D

capo III

F

Cont. rhy. simile

***Gtr. 1**
(Acoustic)

Gtr. 2 *(Acoustic)*

Gtr. 3 *(Electric)*

*Gtr. 1 capo III.

Verse:

1. I was feel - in' the blues, __ I was
I've got - ta say __ that the

Gtr. 3 *(Verse 1 only)*

Gtr. 2

Gtr. 3 *(Verse 2 only)*

P.M. throughout

Two Piña Coladas - 7 - 1
28975

208

Two Piña Coladas - 7 - 2
28975

Chorus:

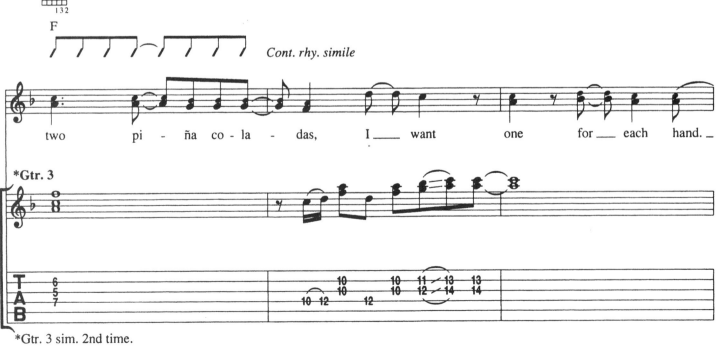

*Gtr. 3 sim. 2nd time.

212

bye to her good-tim-in' man.

Gtr. 2

2. Oh, now

Two Piña Coladas - 7 - 6
28975

UNANSWERED PRAYERS

Words and Music by
LARRY B. BASTIAN,
PAT ALGER and
GARTH BROOKS

216

w/Rhy. Figs. 1 & 1A

Gtr. 3

3. She

Verse 3:

w/Rhy. Figs. 2, 2A & 2B *(1st 7 measures only)*

was-n't quite the an - gel that I re - mem - bered in my dreams, and I could

tell that time had changed me in her eyes too, it seemed. We tried to

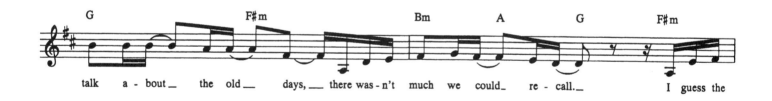

talk a - bout the old days, there was-n't much we could re - call. I guess the

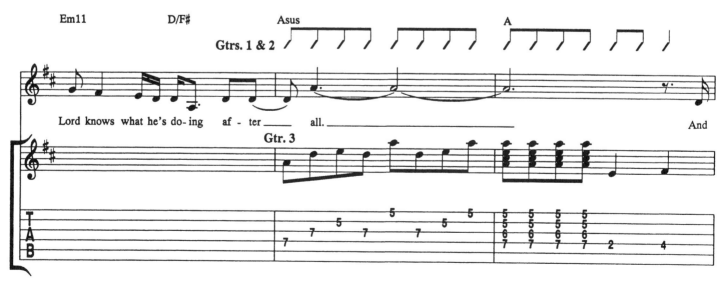

Lord knows what he's do-ing af - ter all. And

Gtrs. 1 & 2

Gtr. 3

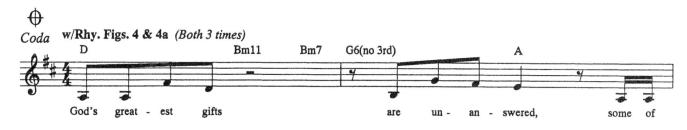

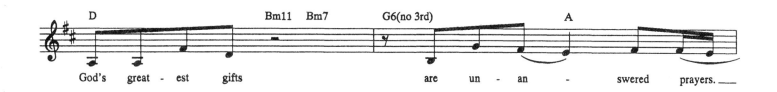

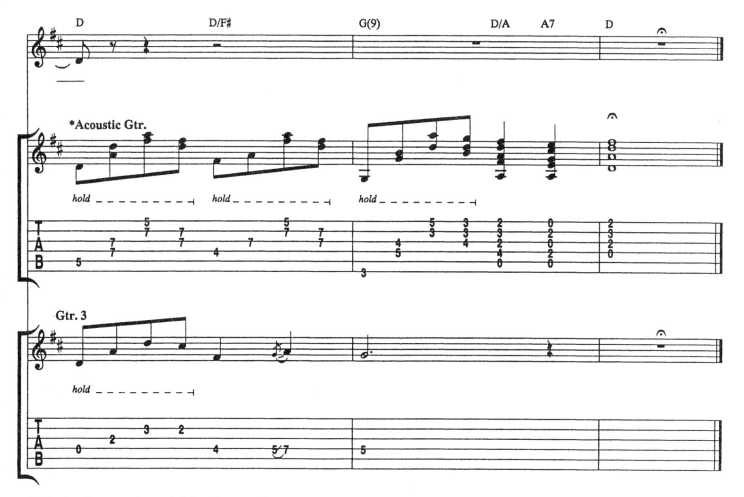

* This acoustic gtr. part is gtrs. 1 & 2 arr. for one guitar.

WE SHALL BE FREE

Words and Music by
STEPHANIE DAVIS
and GARTH BROOKS

Freely ♩ = 68

Intro:
*(G)

(E)

This ain't comin' from no proph-et,

*Chords implied by piano.

(A7sus)   (A7)   (C)   (D9)

just an or - di-nar-y man. _____   But when I

(Em)   (G)   (A7sus)   (A7)

close my eyes I see _____ the way _____ this world _____ shall be _____ when we

rit.

(C)   (D6)   (D9)   (G)   Moderately ♩ = 98

all walk hand _____ in hand. _____   Ooh. _____

Gtr. 2
(Acoustic)   G5

p

Ooh.   Ooh. _____   Ooh. _____   When _____ the

Gtr. 1

f   mf

We Shall Be Free - 13 - 2
28975

224

228

We Shall Be Free - 13 - 7
28975

We Shall Be Free - 13 - 10
28975

232

We Shall Be Free - 13 - 13
28975

WORKIN' FOR A LIVIN'

Words and Music by
HUEY LEWIS and CHRIS HAYES

Workin' for a Livin' - 7 - 1
28975

238

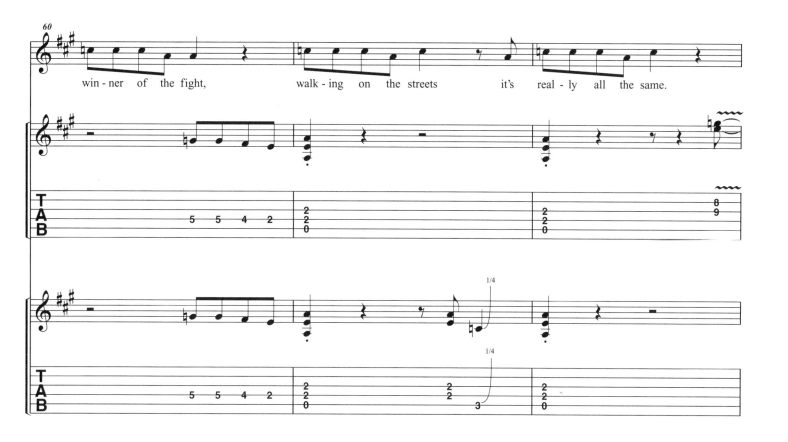

win-ner of the fight, walk-ing on the streets it's real-ly all the same.

Chorus:

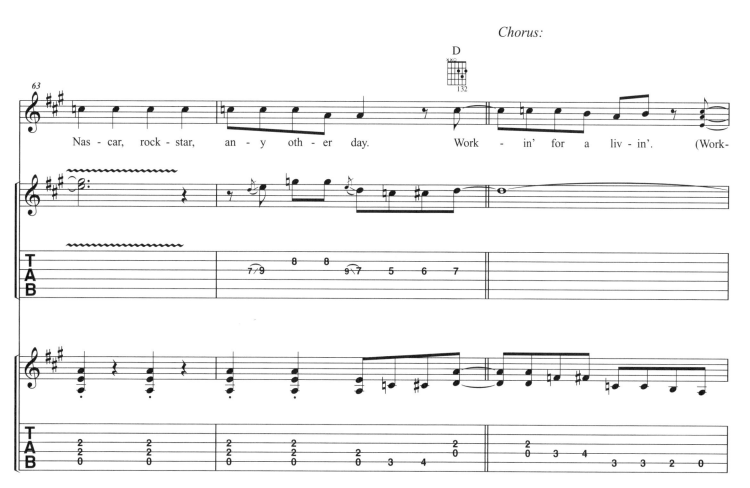

Nas-car, rock-star, an-y oth-er day. Work-in' for a liv-in'. (Work-

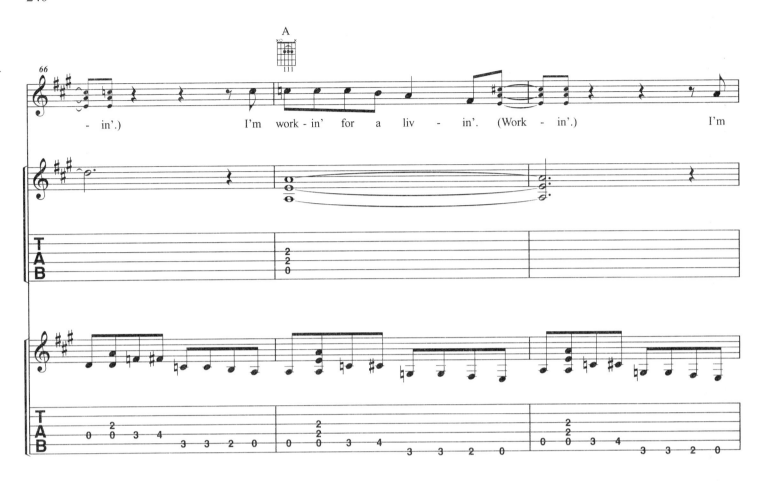

WHAT SHE'S DOING NOW

Words and Music by
PAT ALGER and GARTH BROOKS

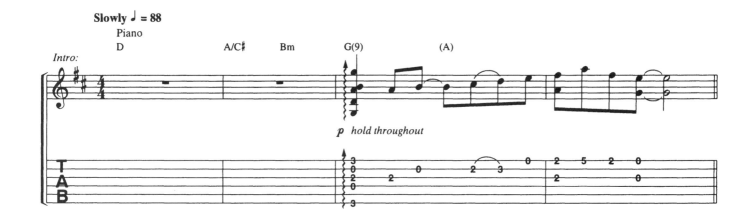

What She's Doing Now - 6 - 1
28975

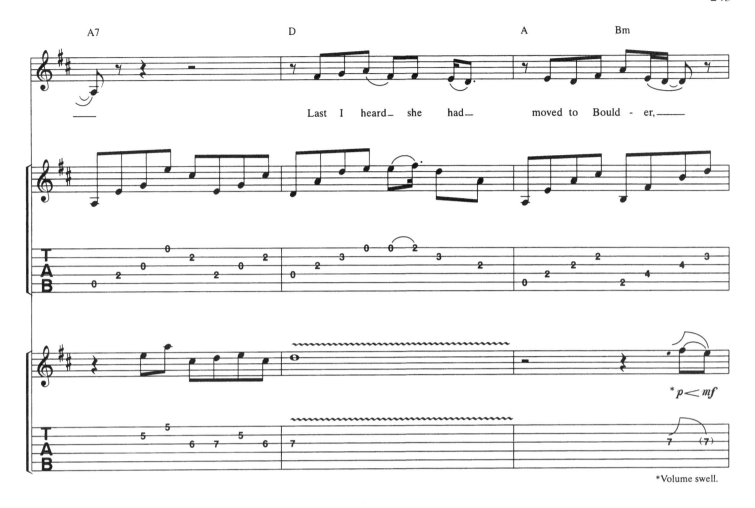

*Volume swell.

Last I heard— she had— moved to Bould-er,—

but where she's now,— I don't— know.— But there's some-thing 'bout— this time—

What She's Doing Now - 6 - 4
28975

Verse 2:
Just for laughs, I dialed her old number,
But no one knew her name.
Hung up the phone, sat there and wondered.
If she'd ever done the same.
I took a walk in the evenin' wind
To clear my head somehow.
But tonight, I lie here thinkin'
What's she doing now?
(To Chorus:)

WHEN YOU COME BACK TO ME AGAIN

Words and Music by
JENNY YATES and GARTH BROOKS

*Chords implied by piano.

Band enters 2nd time

Verses 1 & 2:

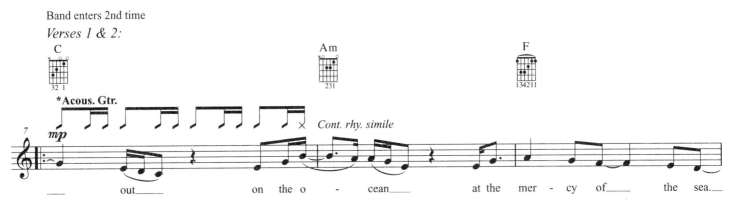

2. *See additional lyrics*

*Acous. Gtr. enter 2nd time.

*Elec. Gtr. enters 2nd time.

When You Come Back to Me Again - 6 - 1
28975

Verse 2:
'Cause there's a lighthouse in a harbor shining faithfully,
Pouring its light out across the water for this shining soul to see
That someone out there still believes in me.
(To Chorus:)

WRAPPED UP IN YOU